296.42
L87f

126139

DATE DUE			

Faith and Destiny of Man

Faith and Destiny of Man

*Traditional Judaism in
a New Light*

by
JOSEPH H. LOOKSTEIN

Bloch Publishing Company
New York

TO GERTRUDE

Who during forty years of happy marriage gave me
all that is most precious in life—wonderful children, a serene home and, above all, her loving
presence at my side.

Foreword

The twenty chapters of this book have been described as "homiletical essays." This designation is not common, and a word of explanation may prove helpful.

An essay is a piece of writing in which the author is concerned primarily with pertinent information on a particular subject. As a rule, though there are many exceptions, the author retains an objectivity and an intellectual detachment. He seeks to convey truth and to transmit enlightenment.

The homiletical essayist desires much more. He not only strives to enlighten, but also to persuade. He uses his art medium not merely to purvey information, but to generate inspiration. Of necessity, even his method is different. For his appeal is not alone to the mind, but to the soul and heart as well.

The essayist is a writer; the homiletical essayist is a preacher. The essayist is guided by the principles of rhetoric; the preacher is motivated by the canons of prophecy. One hopes to educate a person; the other expects to transform a personality.

The homiletical essays in this volume are, therefore, religious discourses, preachments that deal with the situation of man in the twentieth century, with his emotional problems, his intellectual needs and his moral dilemmas. They are especially concerned with the Jew in his relation to the society of which he is a part, to the ancestral faith which is his richest heritage and to the peoplehood of Israel whose destiny he shares.

While the themes of these sermons are influenced by contemporary life, their spirit and substance are drawn from the classic sources of Judaism. Biblical and rabbinic texts are copiously cited. They are made to shed light on the great issues of our day and to provide insights for the perplexing problems of our time. Through them the Jewish tradition speaks to the modern man and the modern Jew.

These sermons were delivered over a number of years before Congregation Kehilath Jeshurun during the High Holiday season. At Kehilath Jeshurun I spent almost all of the forty years of my rabbinate. They were happy and challenging years and, because of the generous cooperation that I received, they were also fruitful and creative years. I am grateful to the Almighty for placing and keeping me at the head of such a superb religious fellowship, and I am grateful to those who comprise that fellowship for all that I enjoyed at their hands.

"Thus shall be my word, which goeth forth from my mouth; it shall not return empty unto me, but it shall accomplish that which I please, and succeed wheresoever I send it." These words from Isaiah represent a Divine charge to prophet and preacher. Every teacher of religion hopes that his words shall not return empty, but shall succeed wheresoever they may reach. This is my humble hope and earnest prayer.

Contents

Part III

BASIC HUMAN NEEDS

Part I

The Old Tradition in a New Light

1

The Old Tradition in a New Light

Our text will probably give little satisfaction and offer feeble persuasion to the modernist mind. Young people are certainly not likely to be pleased with it.

It comes from the farewell address of Moses. Speaking to his people on the threshold of the Promised Land, he said: "Remember the days of old, consider the years of past generations; ask your father and he will inform you, your elders, and they will tell you." [1]

These are dangerous words for our progressive generation, "Remember the days of old." What for? What can they teach this brave new world? Let the historian occupy himself with the musty records of bygone yesteryears. Let the archaeologist dig them up out of long forgotten heaps and abandoned ruins.

"Ask your father . . . your elders . . . ?" What guidance can they offer? Their wisdom might have been adequate for the horse and buggy days. But for the space age? They have little to offer to minds exposed to the benefits of science and

1. Deut. 32:7.

I

for situations governed by new social standards and by fresh ethical outlooks.

So, be off with your days of old! Let the fathers and elders repose in peace and let their traditions remain interred with their bones.

In fairness, however, our modernists ought to admit that their conception of tradition is hardly correct. Tradition is generally represented as the dead hand of the past shackling the powerful arm of the present. Whatever is traditional is antiquated, old and, hence, of course, bad. "History is bunk," said an automobile tycoon in 1919. And the same gibe is frequently hurled at tradition, which is an aspect of history.

Not so, my modernist friend! Not everything that is new is good, and not all that is old is bad. Tradition is not the grit and the rust in the wheels of progress. Not infrequently is it the oil that lubricates those wheels. "A page of history," said Oliver Wendell Holmes, "is worth a volume of logic." And tradition, which is part of the record of history, is of equal worth.

The traditionalist, too, must make an admission. "Remember the days of old," is not the same as "the good old days." The good old days were not at all as good as our nostalgic elders would have us believe. In the good old days there was much evil. There was slavery in the good old days, and tyranny, and idolatry, and paganism. There were "hundred-year wars" in the good old days, and dark ages and inquisitions and religious massacres. I guess that Koheleth summed it up well: "Do not say, 'how was it that the former years were better than these,' for it is not out of wisdom that you ask this." [2]

A further admission might as well be made. Tradition does not mean the ruthless dictatorship of the past, the blind and irrational acceptance of the old, merely because it is old. That is what Henrik Ibsen in his famous play denounced as ghosts of the past. "What we have inherited from our fathers and

2. Eccl. 7:10.

mothers . . . are all sorts of dead ideas and lifeless old beliefs. They have no tangibility but they haunt us all the same, and we cannot get rid of them . . ."

If this is tradition, then we will have nothing of that. Judaism, certainly, will not countenance such a point of view. Judasim emphasizes reason, not blind faith. It stresses understanding, not intellectual surrender; knowledge and inquiry, and not helpless submission. No, for Judaism, at least, tradition is not a voice from the dead which commands, "Obey me!" It is rather the thrilling call of living experience which says, "Use me!"

Having made these admissions, we should be prepared to recognize certain truths about tradition. Unless we recognize these truths we will be only half-correct. We will emancipate ourselves from the dictatorship of the past, but we will become enslaved by the tyranny of the present.

The first truth is that tradition has one decisive advantage. Implicit in the very meaning of the word "tradition" is the fact that it has withstood the test of time. When we deal with a particular tradition, we are not dealing with a whim, a fancy, a current fad or an exploratory experiment. We are dealing with something stable and solid, firm and established. Every great tradition is confirmed by time and endorsed by the experiences of countless generations.

The example that naturally comes to mind is marriage. People, at some stage of human history, discovered that when they married the one person that they loved above all others and whom they loved in a way that they loved no other, their lives were enriched by that union and their souls were uplifted by that love. Husbands and wives discovered bliss in the ineffable bonds that nothing could sever. Their hopes were blended, their personalities fused and the spiritual resources of two individuals were poured into a common pool of human happiness.

Well, shall we cast away this institution of traditional marriage? Some have, you know. One out of every four marriages in our country ends in divorce. Over one hundred thousand children are born out of wedlock every year in America to teen-age mothers. Read the Kinsey report and the shocking statistics on extramarital relations of American males and females. Shall we then give up the institution of marriage? Is there comparable happiness possible in some other alternative?

Of course, marriage is an old institution. But it has withstood the test of generations, the challenges of time and circumstance, the ravages of a thousand catastrophies. It survived recurrent social alternatives like concubinage, polygamy, polyandry, trial marriage, easy divorce, promiscuity and infidelity. Out of all this moral havoc and out of the ashes of wasted lives and blighted homes rose intact this Phoenix, fresh and enduring.

"It is not good for man to be alone, I shall make a helpmate unto him," [3] says Scripture. That's tradition!

"Behold thou are sanctified unto me with this ring according to the law of Moses and Israel." That's tradition!

"He who is without wife is without joy, without blessing and without good," [4] says the Talmud. That's tradition!

Shall we then discard the institution of marriage? It *is* old? Indeed, as old as Adam and Eve! That's a long time. But time from the beginnings of the race attests to its validity.

We may now proceed to a second truth. A tradition properly revered becomes the second nature of man. The continuity of an institution through time conditions those who live by it until it becomes the habitual way of life.

Our actions are, and should be, the result of reason. Our conduct should be motivated by sound logic. Our critical fa-

3. Gen. 2:18.
4. Yeb. 62b.

culties ought to control our behavior and our attitudes toward life. Every sensible traditionalist will concede that.

But life does not always give us a chance to think. Split-second decisions must frequently be made. Emergencies arise and swift action is called for. Temptations in all their evil allurement loom up suddenly. Seductions of every variety cross our path with the speed of a train streaking through the night. And we do not always hear the warning whistle of impending danger.

At such times it is our second nature that comes to the rescue. Habits of a lifetime provide the conditioned reflexes for proper moral responses. When passion takes over, reason is paralyzed. It is then that a great tradition asserts itself; takes over, if you please, and subtly, surreptitiously—yes, perhaps even subconsciously—determines a person's action.

The ancient rabbis explained that when Joseph was tempted by Potiphar's wife, he was saved from moral transgression by the image of his father, Jacob.[5] See what tradition does! A wholesome home, noble ideals learned in childhood, the inspiring example of an upright parent, all combine to provide resistance for a moment of weakness and courage in a moment of challenge.

When the nature of man displays its frailty, when animal appetites and passions threaten the soul, the second nature, cultivated in part by noble traditions, comes to the rescue and man emerges morally intact, spiritually triumphant.

The newspapers once reported that a nine-year-old boy and his eleven-year-old sister fell through the ice on a lake near their home. The rescuer who tried to save them was unable to handle both of them. He later reported that the boy said to him, "Never mind me, save my sister." *

5. Tanhuma 8.
* This illustration is from a brilliant sermon by Harry Emerson Fosdick, entitled "The Power of a Great Tradition."

That nine-year-old boy must certainly have absorbed, through instruction or example, the spirit of a great tradition. It was not reason or logic that spoke his heroic words, "Never mind me, save my sister." It was tradition.

In the trenches of World War I, the tense and huddled soldiers heard the moaning of a wounded comrade caught in the barbed wire of No Man's Land. One of them was about to go "over the top" to his rescue. "I order you not to move," was the command of his officer. "Sorry, Sir, I seem to hear a higher command from a superior officer." And over he went.

Whosoever can hear a higher command at such a time has really heard the echo of a great tradition. These echoes were heard in a thousand fox holes of the last war, and they are still audible in every space capsule that orbits around our planet. They are the great traditions that have become for some personalities their second nature.

This should make many of us who are parents think hard and earnestly. Are we the faithful bearers of the traditions imparted to us, and are we conveying them to our children? Are our homes hospitable to those traditions? The American home is well built, well appointed and well stocked. But what about the spiritual content of our homes? Old Dean Gildersleeve of Barnard, at eighty-five, makes a pertinent comment on the subject. Modern parents, she feels, desire most that "their children be happy every hour of the day—every hour!"

How nice! Happiness is a desirable mood. But happiness to what end? And by what means? Unless proper answers are provided for these questions, our homes will hardly develop great traditions.

"I want my children to have all the things I *didn't* have," says a kind and good-natured father. But alas, not a wise one! So he proceeds to load his children with all kinds of things— generous allowances, charge accounts, convertibles, luxury trips abroad and what not. Are the youngsters happy as a result of this? Is character developed in this way? Are great traditions cultivated in this manner? The record of our day somehow does not show it.

Why should not parents say instead, "we want our children to have what we *did* have." And they had plenty! They had great traditions of love, loyalty and reverence. They knew how to be grateful for the little gifts of life. They found joy in simple pleasures. They practised frugality and understood discipline. They were not afraid of work. Their education was gotten the hard way. College for them was not easy courses, snap subjects, over-indulgence in athletics, playboy fraternities and silly sororities. No wonder that after sixty-two years as an educator Dean Gildersleeve thinks that "education today is pretty poor . . . ," that it "lacks iron and steel . . ." and that "it's kind of flabby."

A further truth now becomes apparent. Tradition not only does not block progress, but is the very essence of progress. This is what our younger people would call "a real switch." But, consider a moment in patience.

You are here this evening, and by your presence you are going back to the "days of old." You are performing devotions, and by doing so you are identifying yourself with an ancient people and with a ritual that goes back three thousand years. You are wearing an old *talith*, a garment which our ancestors wore in ancient Palestine when Homer's heroes were still murdering each other. It is the same *talith* with which our forefathers wrapped themselves as they plunged into the flames of the Inquisition. It is the same *talith*—and there are millions like it—which was found ripped and blood-stained in a thousand desecrated synagogues of Nazi Europe.

You are reading prayers and chants composed by sages two millennia before our era and by martyred poets of the Dark Ages. Yes, you might even shed a tear as you think of all this, the same kind of tear that your grandfather and grandmother let fall, the mark of which you can still recognize on the old prayer book that you cherish as a family heirloom.

Does that mean that we are of a sudden retreating into the dead past? Are we yielding to Ibsen's "lifeless old beliefs?" No, a thousand times no! By returning to tradition you are this day becoming more progressive. You are proclaiming a declaration of interdependence with the past. You are not retreating; you are advancing.

You are sitting next to a father or a mother, and with all your sophistication you would love to embrace them and clasp them to your heart. You are thus recapturing the tradition of family solidarity which is the most precious historic asset of our people and without which our future is dark and uncertain.

You have even finally found courage this day to admit your errors, to "confess your sins" to a God who understands. You are thereby acknowledging the reality of Divine Providence, which is at the core of every religious tradition.

You are fasting this day, depriving yourself of physical pleasures—"afflicting your souls" the Bible calls it—and you are in that way recognizing that life can be spiritual. The world is more than a playground or a cosmic ballroom in which weird dances absorb our energies and leave us tired but unrefreshed. In a word, you are this day asserting that life is a holy opportunity and that man is spiritually equipped to exploit it.

Be not ashamed of what you are doing this day. Let go! Return! For by recapturing your traditional faith, you are not retreating, but advancing.

But even in a larger and more universal sense tradition is very often synonymous with progress. It seems but yesterday when people under the spell of a great aviator and his wife spoke about "the wave of the future." Their argument ran something like this: Democracy has had its chance. The doctrine that all men are created equal had its day in court. The outcome was bad. Man became flabby, mushy, sentimental. Governments became weak and phlegmatic. A new day must come. We need strong men, brave leaders—*Fuehrers!* That was "the wave of the future," the new direction of progress.

Was it? That was man stalking back to the jungle. That was the tom-tom of the savage beating all over again. It cost millions of lives and untold rack and ruin to save and to vindicate democracy. Which was progress, the then new "wave of the future," or the old and traditional democracy?

Come and let us admit it. Every progressive institution that we possess, every great ethical ideal that we cherish, is not new but old. Liberty, democracy, the family, the home, the Ten Commandments, honor, reverence—these are the gifts of tradition and the stepping stones to progress.

Listen to some of this. "Do not hate your brother in your heart . . . nor shall you stand idly by the blood of your neighbor." [6] Speak of brotherhood and inter-racial amity—there it is.

"And they shall beat their swords into ploughshares, and their spears into pruning forks." [7] Speak of world peace—there it is.

"Hath not one God made us, one Father created us? Wherefore shall we deal treacherously with each other?" [8] Speak of the abolition of bigotry—there it is.

Can we improve on all this? Those who live by these ideals, what are they: reactionaries or progressives? Indeed, "Ask your father and he will inform you, your elders, and they will tell you."

Does that suggest that we should reject all that is new; that we should spurn new ideas and fresh insights? No traditional-

6. Lev. 19:16, 17.
7. Isaiah 2:4.
8. Malachi 2:10.

ist in his right mind would even remotely imply that. There
are times when old ways must be abandoned and new paths
must be blazed. There are occasions when we must heed the
divine call: "Get thee out from thy land, from thy birthplace
and from thy father's house into the land whither I will show
thee." To advance is a divine imperative. But if we are to go
forward without going astray, if we are to proceed and arrive, then we need a compass. That compass is tradition.

That compass is indispensable to true progress. It will in-
struct us that in science we should seek the new; in ideals, the
old; in technology, the new; in ethics, the old; in fashions, the
new; in morals, the old.

The immortal Chief Rabbi Kook of Palestine, religious
philosopher and mystic, summed up our thought with remarkable clarity:

> *"Let the old be revived;*
> *Let the new be sanctified."*

2 ❦

What Is the Destiny of Man—
The Answer of Judaism

Our presence here tonight is an admission of our interest in the ultimate ends of life. We feel that life is worth while; so we came to pray for it. We believe that life has meaning and purpose; so we are in a House of God to reflect on it. We recognize that there is an author of life; so we appeal to that Divine Author "to inscribe us in the Book of Life."

But that is only the beginning of the matter. We may agree with the poet that:

> "Life is real! Life is earnest!
> And the grave is not its goal . . ."

But we can still wonder with the philosopher as to what is the goal of life. What *is* the nature of human destiny?

We are not alone in such reflections. Others before us were similarly troubled by the problem of existence. Here, for example, is the Psalmist, pleading: "O, Lord, let me know my end." [1] And here is Job, afflicted in body and troubled in mind, complaining: "What is my strength that I shall hope, and what is mine end that I shall prolong my life." [2]

1. Psalms 39:5.
2. Job 6:11.

From Ecclesiastes to Sartre, from the ancient rabbis to the modern existentialists, thinking men have been preoccupied with the nature, purpose and destiny of life. In one formulation or another they all asked for the same thing: "O, Lord, let me know my end."

While a discussion of this problem is, as we have seen, timeless and universal, it has become especially important for our generation. Life was never more incomprehensible. Existence was never more uncertain. Human effort and striving never appeared so purposeless. Professor Whitehead speaks of us as "the incommensurable idiots of the universe."

His unflattering estimate of us is not easily refuted. Two major wars in one generation, and a third by no means impossible! The world has become a huge arsenal in which nuclear weapons predominate. Mankind is hopelessly divided by an impenetrable iron curtain with tyranny on one side of it and fear on the other. We have reason to ponder the problem of our destiny. "O, Lord, let me know my end."

There are, of course, some who are not concerned with this at all. Their view of the universe and their evaluations of life do not require a solution to the problem of human destiny. Life to them is just a series of accidents. Existence is a fortuitous intermeshing of circumstances. Human conduct is not volitional. It is the result of stray moods, lucky breaks, daring gambles. Man is a driven leaf, tossed about by the frivolous winds of chance and wafted hither and yon by the capricious currents of circumstance. His birth is a biologic accident, his life a mere lingering and his death a dissolution into nothingness. He enters upon the stage of existence without a worth-while script; he performs without benefit of director; he makes his exit without the thrill of applause.

What is man's destiny according to such a view of life? What can it be when there is no divine law but a statistical law of probability? What can it be when man is a mere organism and love is but a flushing of the glands? What can it be when a mother's tear is but a chemical compound and a father's grief is a physical grimace? What can man's destiny be in such a universe?

Let a representative of this view speak for himself and his fellows. "Man is forlorn because neither within him nor without does he find anything to cling to." These are the words of Jean-Paul Sartre. Well, if there is nothing to cling to, Mr. Sartre, then man cannot be propelled forward nor can he climb upward. And since he cannot stand still, then his destiny is to drop downward—downward into the abyss.

There is another view of life with its insight into human destiny. Here is how it goes.

Man might have been a perfect creature. His life might have remained untouched by sin. Eternal life might have been his destiny. But . . . once upon a time there was a man called Adam and a woman called Eve. They lived together blissfully in a Garden of Eden. All of a sudden a wicked dragon in the form of a slimy serpent invaded their blissful abode. There was no gallant knight to slay this dragon, so Adam and Eve succumbed to his wiles and yielded to the temptation of violating God's command. They lived unhappily ever after.

By the act just described, which is known in theology as Original Sin, all the children of men lost, one might say, their destiny, and were doomed to predestination. Man became predisposed to evil, to sin, to depravity and to ultimate death. Imbedded, as it were, in his nature was the seed of evil that sends forth its tortuous vines to strangulate the human will and to smother the human personality. The best man can hope for is to wash away the effects of Original Sin by the waters of baptism and to hope to achieve, through faith, ultimate salvation in the world to come.

Almost all the Fundamentalist forms of Christianity subscribe to this doctrine. Originally proposed by Paul, adapted by Luther, expanded by Calvin, it can still be recognized, though in modern dress, in the thinking of Kierkegaard and the other religious existentialists.

Man's destiny, according to this view, is offered little latitude. His fate is sealed. His future is predetermined. The die of his character is cast.

One would expect that at the hands of modern sociology man would get a better deal. Surprisingly, he doesn't. The anthropologist in this respect is no different from the Fundamentalist, except that his vocabulary is different. "Neither as groups nor as individuals do we have a choice of roles or fates . . ." says a famous anthropologist. "What a man thinks, feels and does is determined by his culture . . ." says another. He may not be a doomed "sinner in the hands of an angry God," but he is nonetheless doomed to be what culture decrees, what environment dictates, what heredity determines.

Man, according to these views, simply cannot be himself. He is offered no choice. He is what his ancestry made him. He behaves as his environment conditions him, as his hungers demand, as his appetites dictate. He is never the master of his destiny, nor the captain of his soul.

Is it any wonder that so many recoil from such a view and rebel against a world in which it prevails? If Professor Whitehead can speak of us as "the incommensurable idiots of the world," what can you expect of a "beatnik," except to behave like an idiot.

Why are we surprised at the rebellions on college campuses? Why are we shocked when the analyst's couch has become the symbol of our generation? Why are we astounded when an army of intellectuals—Jewish and non-Jewish—have virtually resigned from the human race and have become a legion of the "alienated" and a company of "outsiders?"

If man is a mere puppet in the hands of fate; if he is only a dummy bouncing helplessly on the knee of a ventriloquist—divine or human; if he is a mechanical tool in the manipulative fingers of destiny; if he is all that, and yet is endowed with a soul, a mind and a conscience, then he is doomed to be a neurotic, and worse.

It is, therefore, gratifying for a teacher of Judaism to find in the Jewish tradition comfort and hope for confused and bewildered people, for a distracted and perplexed generation. What, according to Judaism, is the destiny of man? How does Judaism react to the Psalmist's prayer: "O, Lord, let me know my end."

First and foremost, Judaism declares that man is a free agent. He is endowed by God with a most precious gift—the gift of freedom of will. He has a right to choose his course in life, without direction from above or interference from below. Neither God nor the devil is master over his choice. "I call heaven and earth to testify that I have set before you this day, life and death, blessing and curses; do thou *choose* life." [3]

These are the parting words of Moses ere he left his people. They are the Emancipation Proclamation of the individual. They broke man's chains and gave him freedom of thought, of choice and of action. They conferred upon him human dignity and full sovereignty over his personal and social conduct.

The sages of the Talmud further elaborated on this doctrine of freedom of choice. "Everything is in the hands of God, except the fear of God." [4] Many things are preordained, say the Rabbis, but not the decision to be righteous or wicked. [5] Man's conduct is, of course, of concern to God, but it is the business of man.

3. Deut. 30:19.
4. Ber. 33b.
5. Nida 16b.

Every Jew in his personal life, and the Jewish people collectively, lived by this doctrine. Our very survival is the result of our determination to live by *our* standards, according to *our* traditions, in keeping with *our* ideals and by the light of *our* values. What would have been our fate had we allowed our environments—they were always in the plural—to rule us. Where would we be today if we permitted the cultures all about us to engulf us, the ghettos to strangle us, Christianity and Islam to convert us, the endless inquisitions and pogroms to scare us and the gas chambers of our day to suffocate us.

Individually and collectively we looked death in the face a thousand times. We resisted paganism. We battled Hellenism. We preached freedom and justice and peace. All this we did for millennia through prophet and sage, through lawgiver and Psalmist. We did all this because we would not surrender to idolatry, to immorality, to brutality, to slavery and to savagery.

We did not succumb to the environment. We met it head on and triumphed over it. Then came the payoff in our day. Auschwitz! Treblinka! Buchenwald! All the extermination infernos of a continent turned into a jungle!

Even then we were not crushed. At the clearing of crematoria we locked hands and chanted a dirge of death with overtones of hope and faith. "I believe," we chanted, and heaving mass graves trembled at our elegy, "I believe in the coming of the Messiah."

And the Messiah did come, in the form of a Jewish State and a liberated and triumphant people. *We* determined our destiny, and God confirmed and blessed our determination.

This is the saga of our people. This is the odyssey of our faith. Will our Jewish intellectuals resign from that? Will they turn their backs on a faith which, alone among all faiths, exalts the individual and entrusts to him the fate and destiny of the world?

But the Jewish tradition does not stop at this point. For above the Jewish doctrine of free will, there is a corollary doctrine. Not alone is man free to choose without God's dictation; he can even cause God to revise his decision.

"The Holy One, blessed be He, decrees," say our wise men in the Talmud, "but the righteous may nullify the decree." [6] Think of that. What religion bestows such prerogatives upon man?

What is our entire philosophy of penitence if not a pious assertion that our fate is never sealed, that the gates of heaven are never shut to our prayers and that the eyes of God continue to search for evidence of our remorse. "Penitence, Prayer and Charity will avert the evil decree." Is not that the never-ending refrain and the basic theme of the High Holiday season?

A beautiful tale to illustrate this viewpoint is recounted in the Talmud. The sages were engaged in acrimonious debate. Some ruled one way; others decided another way. One of the disputants arose and in passion exclaimed: "Let heaven declare that my decision is correct." A heavenly voice responded accordingly. The vote was taken and the ruling went contrary to the heavenly opinion. The tale continues that the Divine comment on the action of the rabbinic judges was: "My children have overruled me! My children have overruled me!" [7]

To overrule God on human destiny is a prerogative that Judaism alone awards to man. *L'homme propose et Dieu dispose*, says the French anecdote. Our grandmothers in their simple faith used to put it even more quaintly. *"Der mensch tracht und Gott lacht."* Not quite, sainted grandmother. There is more power vested in man than you dared imagine.

6. This statement appears in various formulations in the Talmud: viz. (M.K. 16b; Sab. 63a; B.M. 63a). It is best stated in the Introduction to the Zohar, Section 10, where it reads: The Holy One issues decrees and the righteous men of Israel nullify them.
7. The entire episode is narrated in full detail in Baba Mezia 59a.

Our tradition has a further thought on this problem of human destiny. Here it is. If man has the right to choose, then he also has the obligation to choose right.

Judaism does not permit man to evade personal responsibility. It will not allow him to cast blame upon his forbears. What do we say in our confessional? "For we are not so brazen and hardened as to say to you . . . we are righteous and sinless; but verily, *we* and our ancestors have sinned."

We do not deny the influence of heredity upon the physical and mental character of an individual. But are we not carrying it too far? Let us stop blaming our grandmothers for our complexes, our mothers for our rages and our fathers for our aggressions. The wounds and lacerations inflicted upon our personalities by others are many and painful. But at some point in our lives we mature and become men and women. It is then that we must discover or be shown the powers and potentials that reside within us. It is then that we must recognize our right to choose and our responsibility to choose right.

Nor will Judaism permit us to throw the blame entirely upon our environment. "The place does not bring honor to the man; it is man who brings honor to the place." [8] Great men and great gangsters emerged from slums. Heroes and cowards developed on the same battlefields. Lawgivers and law breakers came from the same Egypt. Sluggish Eskimos and adventurous explorers were produced by the same frozen wastes. To be sure, environment is a factor in personality development. But man is capable of resisting, conquering and creating his environment.

Recall the story of the preacher who spoke to the Gaon of Vilna. It is not difficult, he told him, to become a Gaon of Vilna when one is secluded in his own home, hermetically sealed off from his environment and insulated against the

8. Taanith 21b.

problems and temptations of life. Go out into the market place, said the preacher, and if you can still remain the saint that you are, you will have demonstrated true greatness. And it has been done!

This lesson is important for our day. We have become naively psychiatry-minded. There is a tendency to explain away the criminal and to whitewash the guilty. The Communist is a neurotic. The war criminal, with the blood of millions on his hands, had an unhappy childhood. The lewd and promiscuous woman is the product of parental repression. The dishonest politician was brought up in poverty. And in all this diagnosis of smut and sin, we lost our awareness of the factor of personal responsibility. We dare not come to regard the analyst's couch as a modern altar of absolution.

"O, Lord, let me know my end." What destiny awaits me as a man? As a Jew? What is the fate of the society of which I am a part?

The answer was given long ago. For once before, according to our sages, such questions were asked of God. His answer was: "Why do you ask Me? Let us go down and ask Man." [9] Indeed, the answer does lie with *us*.

9. Deut. R. II, 9.

3&

Man Without a Capital "M"

Plato is said to have defined man as a two-legged animal without feathers. Diogenes brought a plucked fowl into the Academy and said, "This is Plato's man." The definition was thereupon revised by the addition of these words, "with broad nails."

Whether this story is or is not true is not important. What is important is the recognition that a definition of man is not easily arrived at. Man's oldest and greatest puzzle is man. Long before Plato, the Psalmist wondered, "What is man that thou art mindful of him . . . ?"

Many have been the answers to this question, many the attempts to arrive at a comprehension of the nature and the essence of man. And the quest continues; the puzzle remains unsolved. "What is man that thou art mindful of him?"

What are some of the answers to that question? Here is the most cynical. Man is a little bundle worth approximately $31.04. At that, the price is probably inflationary because phosphates at the moment happen to be costly.

It sounds flippant, does it not? Yet as serious a thinker as Robert Ingersoll phrased it no less flippantly when he said that man is a machine into which we put what is called food and produce what we call thought.

What a flattering definition of man! Man is a machine, a web of cylinders which absorb, digest and assimilate. To be sure, he is a thinking machine, a sort of Univac, but his ultimate destiny is still the junk pile. Poor David! How let down he would have felt had that been the answer to his query, "What is man that thou art mindful of him?"

And what is man according to the insights of the new psychology? He is a creature of libido, a bundle of passions, a coil of complexes, a lump of inhibitions. Turn him inside out and one can still see the pronounced traces of his primitive ancestry and of his beastly origins. If some triumphant personalities, past or contemporary, do not correspond to that image, their non-resemblance is purely accidental.

Even some religions do not handle man more charitably. Fundamentalist doctrine and crisis theology regard man as a tool in the manipulative hands of an angry God. By predestination his whole life's course is mapped out for him. Born against his will, man staggers on without intelligible purpose, spinning out life's fabric upon a loom not of his choice, and after a pattern not of his making.

What, then, is man according to such religion? He is an automaton, a robot bomb hurled into space by some invisible hand and landing upon this planet as a sort of human dud.

This leads us straight to our first positive and affirmative statement on the nature of man. For such a statement, I turn to the Jewish tradition. Man, according to Judaism, is not a tool; he is the mechanic. He is not an instrument of life but its artisan. He is not the product of fate but its master. "Monarch of the universe," is what the Zohar, repository of Jewish mysticism, calls him. Monarch, mind you, not subject! King, not underling!

Scripture confirms and punctuates this view. "Thou gavest him dominion over all the works of Thy hand. Thou hast put all things under his feet." Man, then, is the master over the world's resources and the custodian of all its riches. He is not God's bellhop; he is God's ambassador. "And thou hast made him but little lower than the angels and thou has crowned him with glory and honor."

Someone must be wondering by now as to what difference all this makes. Who cares about a definition of man? Why be concerned with all this empty speculation as to the nature and essence of man?

It makes a great deal of difference. What man feels he is, will determine how he will behave. If he is a mechanistic contraption racing madly over the tortuous course of life, then he is headed for crash after crash and will end up dangling helplessly at the rear end of the towing truck of destiny. If he is "but little lower than the angels," then his goal is to become angelic. An unworthy definition of man is more than metaphysics. It involves morals. What we think of ourselves will determine what we will make of ourselves.

Our own generation was witness to the consequences of an unworthy definition of man. Man, the "monarch of the universe," became the abject slave of the state—Soviet or Nazi. Upon man was performed the most brutal plastic surgery imaginable. The image of God was eradicated and the mask of the Blond Beast was plastered over his countenance. Love and mercy were excised from the human heart and the venom of hate and savagery was injected in their place. A new definition of man was advanced, a mean and monstrous definition. Man is the tool of the dictator, the puppet of the Fuehrer, the lackey and victim of the tyrant. In consequence, we saw, reenacted before our very eyes, the shocking spectacle of the Fall of Man.

We recall the Eichmann trial and we read the evidence of the current Auschwitz trials and we are numbed. What arguments does the defense advance? What explanations do the defendants offer for brutality, torture and death? The monotonous and melancholy refrain is, "We were merely carrying out orders." Man ceased to be man and became an automaton. He was no longer even a *thinking* machine, Mr. Robert Ingersoll, just a machine. The "monarch of the universe" was transformed into a ventriloquist's dummy bouncing grotesquely on the knee of the devil.

How does Judaism regard such behavior? Will it not absolve one of guilt where obedience to a higher authority is involved? Suppose the mightiest king of Israel were to command a Jew to slay another. Suppose the highest temporal authority, under the threat of death, ordered a person to commit murder. The unanimous opinion of Jewish law is—*Yehoreg v'al ya'avor:* "Let him die and not transgress." Man's responsibility as a man never ends. He cannot abdicate his manliness. He cannot renounce his humanity. *Adam muad l'olam:* "Man is always forewarned." He can never resign from the human species.

Possessed of supreme manliness, endowed with special virtues, man can even stand up to God. This is what Moses did when he insisted that God forgive his people, "And if not, blot me out from thy book . . ." This is what Abraham did when he pleaded for Sodom, ". . . Will you destroy the righteous with the wicked. . . . Shall not the Judge of all the world act with justice?" This is what every sage and saint did in an hour of crisis and peril. "God decrees and the *zadik* annuls the decree."

This is man, as Judaism defines him, as every true religion defines him. "Thou hast made him but little lower than the angels, and hast crowned him with glory and honour."

Men who correspond to this image are not numerous. They are not mass produced. They have to be individually cultivated. They are not rolled off the assembly line of school, state or society. They cannot be prefabricated; they must be custom-made.

Let us face it. Our day, alas, is not geared to develop great souls. Our social and educational machinery is simply not tooled for it. Great scientists, yes! Great athletes, yes! Great tycoons, yes! But not great souls!

There is a variety of reasons for that. For one thing, ours is an age of bigness and not of greatness. Justice Brandeis diagnosed it properly when he called it "the curse of bigness." We have "big" business, "big" labor, "big" budgets, "big" universities, "big" cities. We have become quantity minded and are no longer quality minded.

This has led to an emphasis upon things and possessions rather than upon people. Robert Taft, Jr. recently put it very aptly when he said that, "property rather than person was placed upon the pedestal of pride." Our contemporary vocabulary tells the story. We speak of the number of hands that are employed. Hands, not people! We are concerned with man-power and man-hours but not with man. Man has been totally eclipsed. He has become a number, a statistic, a mute figure on a curve of distribution.

Character and individuality cannot develop in such a climate. Great souls cannot breathe and grow in the oppressive atmosphere of bigness. Saints do not develop in the shadow of skyscrapers.

In addition to the curse of bigness, there is the mixed blessing of modern technology. In a technological civilization the major concern is with machines and not people, with profits and not personalities, with success and not character. Man's uniqueness and individuality are of no account. As a matter of fact, man becomes almost useless and can well be written off. It is one of the paradoxes of our day that the genius of man has made man expendable.

To be sure, it is easier to live in a technological age. There are more comforts and conveniences. There are more commodities to enjoy, more pleasures to indulge in. Life is easier, but is it better?

There are some five million arrests in the United States every year. Juvenile delinquency is mounting alarmingly. We spent about five billion dollars on liquor last year in America, and about a million and a half were arrested for drunkenness. We have the highest standard of living in the world, and we also have almost two million divorces every year. Colloquially put, "we never had it so good"—and never behaved so badly.

No, our age is not conducive to character development. Man is squelched. His individuality is no longer respected. If he is a non-conformist, he is an egg-head. If he does not follow the crowd, he is a loner. If he does not subscribe to the accepted mold, he is a radical. If he shows symptoms of saintliness, he is abnormal.

At this moment some lovely sentiments of the High Holiday liturgy come to mind. Our prayers deal with the Coronation of God; yet man remains their central theme. Our prayers speak of men and nations; yet man in the singular is their primary target. They recount the annals of universal history, but they do not avoid personal biography as well.

Who are the focal characters of Rosh Hashanah? People! Abraham, Isaac, Sarah, Hagar, Ishmael, Abimelech—these men and women and their problems engage our attention. What are some of the fascinating tales that we read this day out of Scripture? Do we read a tractate on abstract philosophy, or a volume on theoretical ethics, or a folio on principles of society? No! We read about a barren Hannah who longed for a child; about an unhappy Sarah and her domestic problem; about a child dying of thirst in a wilderness, while a helpless mother looked on; about an only son whose father was prepared to offer him upon the altar.

Yes, it is about people that we read. People of flesh and

blood! People subject to passion and temptation! People with anxieties and frustrations! People who can stumble and rise again! People who are capable of being a little less than angels and who may be crowned with glory and honour!

On this day, the Jew says to his God, "Thou openest the chronicle of the ages . . . yet the signature of *every* man is in it. . . . A mighty trumpet is sounded, but even a small, still voice is heard." The signature of every man, irrespective of status, of race or of color, must be included in the chronicle of the ages, else it is incomplete. The small, still voice must be heard, else the symphony of life remains unfinished.

The importance of man in the singular ought to be readily acknowledged, in particular by our generation. We, more than any other generation, have seen the heights to which man can rise and the depths to which he can sink.

One man brought our world to the brink of destruction. One man threatened to stampede mankind back to the jungle. One man dropped an iron curtain and split the world in two, with terror and hate on one side and fear and suspicion on the other. One man is at this very moment preventing peace in the Middle East and threatening the security of the world. One man snuffed out the life of a young and brilliant president of unlimited promise to his country and the world.

Now, for the other side of the picture. One man and then another called a halt to the dangers and ravages of crippling infantile paralysis. The genius of one man working alone or with colleagues unlocked the secrets of the atom and unleashed power and energy which if constructively harnessed can save the world. One man conceived the formulas and equations which became the Theory of Relativity and enabled us to penetrate the mysteries and vastnesses of outer space.

How true are our prayers! The chronicle of the ages does have the signature of every man in it. And in the din and clamor of life, one can discern the small still voice even of the most soft-spoken.

In one of his writings, the great preacher, Dr. Harry Emerson Fosdick, reports a conversation between an astronomer and a philosopher. Says the astronomer, "Astronomically speaking, what is man?" The question is understandable. When we think of the staggering dimensions of the universe; when we contemplate the size and distances of the stars; when we reflect upon the speed of light—186,000 miles per second; how natural it is to ask, "Astronomically speaking, what is man?"

And here is the humble answer of the philosopher: "Astronomically speaking, man is the astronomer." It is in man's mind that all these distances have meaning. It is his brain that computes and calculates. It is his genius that wrests the secrets out of the universe. It is his curiosity that grapples with them. And it is his determination that conquers them and transforms them into blessings for the world. Aye, astronomically speaking, man *is* the astronomer.

This, then, is the *religious* definition of man. Man is master; let him never be enslaved. Man is the inventor; let him never be identified with or eclipsed by the machine which is his invention. Man is mind; let his genius never be shackled. Man is prophet; let his vision remain ever clear.

> *"What a piece of work is man,"* says Shakespeare.
> *"How noble in reason; how infinite in faculty; . . .*
> *In action how like an angel;*
> *In apprehension how like a god."*

Well put, indeed! But centuries earlier, David put it even better:

"When I consider Thy heavens, the work of Thy fingers,
The moon and the stars which Thou hast established;

*What is man that Thou art mindful of him and the son of man
That Thou thinkest of him;
For Thou hast made him but little lower than the angels,
And hast crowned him with glory and honour."*

4 ॐ

How Much Is a Man Worth

The author of a recent best-seller concerned himself with the problem of status in our society. As he surveyed one corner of the social scene, he concluded that ". . . any reward system that year after year pays a wailing crooner approximately one hundred times as much as the Chief Justice of the United States Supreme Court is somewhat out of balance." [1]

There is no need to be that diplomatic. There is something radically wrong with the standard of value that prevails in our civilization. What is the relative worth of a crooner and a chief justice, a college football coach and the chairman of its department of philosophy, an atomic scientist and a television performer? How much really is a man worth? So much hinges on the answer to that question.

This question may well occupy us on this holy night. If there is a moment when we stand in stark spiritual nakedness before God, it is on Kol Nidre Night. At other times we may imitate; this night we dare to be genuine. Throughout the year we can pretend; on Kol Nidre Night we should attempt sincerity. Always we are aware of our strength, our importance and our power. Tonight we are conscious of our frailty, our inadequacy and our dependence. "What are we; what is

1. Packard, Vance; *The Status Seekers*, p. 113.

our life; . . . what is our strength; what is our power." The moment is, indeed, appropriate to ask: how much *is* a man worth?

For some, of course, that question was never difficult to answer. An employer, for example, found it relatively simple to determine the worth of a man. How much time did a man give to his labor? How much did he produce? That is how much he is worth. Jacob, in biblical times, tried to explain to Laban how much he meant to him in faithful and loyal performance. Laban, in the characteristic manner of employers of all time, responded: "State your wages and I will pay them." [2] Transposing it into the idiom of our day, it would sound like this: My estimate of your worth is indicated by what I put into your pay envelope. "He is a fifty dollar a week clerk," we say of one. Or, "he is a ten thousand dollar a year man," we say of another. And we leave it at that.

The labor economist also found little trouble in his effort to evaluate man. He appraised the labor market and then computed the worth of man on the basis of the infallible laws of supply and demand.

Then came Karl Marx and introduced yet another dimension by which to measure the worth of man. "From each according to his abilities; to each according to his needs," was the new formula. Price indexes and cost-of-living differentials had to be calculated. Man's worth was then expressed by what he needed and by what his circumstances required him to have.

The Marxian formula represented an advance in the process of evaluating man's worth. At first man was a mere tool, and his price was whatever he, as a tool, produced. Then he became a commodity and subject, therefore, to the impersonal laws of economics. Marx promoted man to the level of an intelligent animal with needs—an animal which eats, grows, reproduces and dies. Quite a promotion!

2. Gen. 30:25.

Are we prepared to accept any of these estimates as the true and real worth of man? If we are, then listen to this. For composing the Ninth Symphony, Beethoven received the equivalent of one hundred and fifty dollars. Was that his worth? For writing Paradise Lost, Milton received from his publisher eighteen English pounds. Was that his worth? Dr. Flemming received nothing but the Nobel Prize for discovering penicillin. And Moses, according to our sages, received as his compensation the chips of granite that fell from the tablets that he carved.[3] Was that his worth? No, some other estimate is necessary. A material standard of values will not do.

The other standard of value must be qualitative in character rather than quantitative, moral rather than material. It will estimate man, not by how much he makes, but by how much he contributes, not by what he *has*, but by what he *is*. Perhaps the adjective, *religious*, can best describe such a standard of value.

As we move toward such a standard of value, we arrive at our first conclusion. It is necessary to distinguish between compensation and worth. Compensation is invariably determined by external factors—supply and demand, cost-of-living conditions and the like. Worth is determined by internal factors—quality of mind, disposition of heart, character of soul, objectives of life. "This man is worth his weight in gold," is a common expression. Nonsense! What we mean is that this man is entitled to receive his weight in gold. His worth may be nothing at all. On the other hand, you may have a humble man whose take-home pay is only what the minimum wage law provides. But he takes it to a home in which there is happiness; he gives it to a wife for whom he has deep love; and out of it he rears a family of happy and well-adjusted children. *This* man is worth his weight in gold.

"When you eat of the labor of your hands, happy and for-

3. Ned. 38a.

tunate will you be. Your wife shall be like a fruitful vine within your house, your children like olive plants round about your table." This is a portrait of a man of worth.

A street sweeper in Tel Aviv once provided a moving illustration of this thought. He had prepared for engineering. A disabling illness made that profession impossible. He, therefore, turned to sweeping streets in the city of Tel Aviv. "But," said he, "my profession is really that of a health officer. I remove dirt, disease and germs, so that the air of this city may be clean, so that little children may breathe it and grow up to be healthy and fine Jews." Will the take-home pay of this man indicate his true worth?

The distinction between compensation and worth is crucial to our entire way of life. When a ceiling is reached on wages, as it is about to be reached, will a man's worth be frozen at that point? When the picket line becomes obsolete, will man's forward march come to an end? When the expense account of a highly paid executive reaches the optimum, will there be no further goals to attain? If all our rewards will be expressed in material well-being, what will happen to our souls? If compensation becomes synonymous with worth, what will be the complexion of our society? If what a man makes becomes more important than what a man is, what will happen to human dignity? What kind of children will we raise; what sort of values will they cherish; what moral climate will they live in? There simply must be a higher standard of value in our life.

If we acknowledge this, then we may proceed to a further conclusion. There are certain efforts and services which cannot possibly be translated into material terms at all. How much was the man worth who invented the wheel and who set the machinery of civilization in motion from the oxcart to the supersonic jet? What was the worth of the man who kindled the first spark and ignited the flame that has kept life aglow? What should have been the salary of the microbe hunters who tracked down invisible bacteria and viruses to their deadly lairs? What should be the take-home pay of the inventors of antibiotics? What reward for the artist who painted Mona Lisa; the genius who sculptured Moses? What shall be the salary of a teacher, just a plain, ordinary primary school teacher, who teaches a child to read and thus opens his eyes to all the possibilities of life? How shall we compensate the surgeon who saves life, the religious teacher who transforms life, the scientist who probes the mystery of life, the artist who enriches life, the jurist who regulates life?

Can there be adequate material reward for these? What standard will be used; what index will be utilized; what formula will be employed? Can't we see that there is, indeed, a higher standard of value. These servants of society do have their reward. Their compensation may be meagre, but they will find a reward that surpasses all compensation, and they will achieve a worth that transcends all material return.

Recall that Moses, according to our sages, received the chips of granite that fell from the tablets that he carved. That was his compensation. Now what was his reward? Say our wise men: "A mine of precious stones and diamonds did God uncover for Moses within his tent, and from that did he obtain his wealth." [4] Yes, Moses found wealth within his own tent. His deep communion with God, his emancipation of a slave people, his giving of divine commandments to mankind and a moral law to the world—these acts were for him a veritable mine of precious wealth, incalculable in its value. Greater reward can come to no man.

Some time ago the press greeted a famous pediatrician, whose test saved countless children from the dread disease of diphtheria. The greeting was delivered to him in the name of

4. J. Shekalim 5:2.

one million children whose lives he is reputed to have saved. There is no compensation for such service. But the lives of a million children—what a reward!

There is, indeed, a higher standard of value in life. But those who live by it do not as a rule enjoy our admiration. We regard them, often with pity, sometimes with scorn. We refer to them as eggheads, long-haired intellectuals, brain trusters, impractical idealists. Our type is the "man in the gray flannel suit," the dynamic executive, the prosperous man of affairs. The manufacturer of a high-priced car displayed an interesting advertisement recently.[5] It showed an actress pointing to the enormous taillights of an automobile and saying, "They let the people behind you know you are ahead of them." What a commentary on a sense of value! The only way to demonstrate that one is ahead is by flashing taillights.

This leads us directly to the next conclusion. A higher standard of value will compel us to revise our definition of success. The success stories of our day are monotonous in their materialistic emphasis. One general theme runs through them all—a junk peddler who became a fabulous oil man; a poor small-town boy who became an industrial tycoon; a newspaper boy who took over a railroad. Are these the only successful people? By what standard is success measured? "This man is worth a million dollars," we say. What we really mean is that he *has* a million dollars. He may not be worth a nickel. By what principles does he live? Is he a person of integrity? How did he make his million? What sort of husband is he; what kind of a father? Unless these questions are answered favorably, our paragon of success may be a dismal and tragic failure.

One of the consequences of the modern success cult is a new phenomenon which has appeared in our society. Vance Packard gave it a name—the Status Seekers. The rationale be-

5. Packard, Vance: *The Status Seekers*, p. 313.

hind this phenomenon is simple. Not all of us can achieve material success. We, therefore, try to act as though we did achieve it. The sun of prosperity simply does not shine upon all of us alike. We, therefore, resort to "Man Tan."

Since not all of us can attain success, we at least try to acquire the symbols of success. We go shopping for those symbols. Sometimes our efforts are harmless, even if they are laughable. We cannot afford a very high-priced car; then we buy a cheaper but glamorous imitation. We look for what is known as a "good address." We join a country club which we cannot always afford. We move into an exclusive neighborhood which is beyond our means. Twenty-five thousand Americans change their residences annually because of that reason. We live by appearances, in the vain hope that we will achieve the *status* of success if only we can flash the symbols of success.

We impress false values upon our children. We make them think that the sparkle and the glitter of life is the true complexion of life. Nothing but an exclusive college will do for our young, and we will exert every pressure to get them into it. We are proud when our son "makes" an exclusive fraternity, and we are heartbroken if our daughter is not "rushed" by a fashionable sorority. We are always looking for the "right" things for our children—the right private school, the right boarding school, the right college, the right friends. But by "right" we invariably mean that which will further status, and status in our minds is invariably linked with success.

Let then a teacher of religion say to people on a holy night like this, that snobbery is an ugly caricature of success; that false status is not true worth; that social climbing is a grotesque exercise and should be shunned by decent people.

This false gospel of success is one of the most pernicious evils of our day. It is especially so because there are other models of success that we can glorify. How about an immigrant tailor's son, Jonas Salk, who attended, not an Ivy League school, but a municipal college, and became the inventor of a vaccine against polio? How about a sickly youngster, Felix Frankfurter, who won scholarship upon scholarship till he attained a distinguished professorship of law and then a respected place in the Supreme Court of our land? How about a rail splitter who became president and a crippled leader who led mankind to its "rendezvous with destiny." How about a Moses who, though "slow of speech and halting of tongue," enunciated truths by which all humanity lives? And how about the legions of humble folk who did not go "from rags to riches," but who did justice, loved mercy and walked humbly with their God. These, too, are models of success. Let us hold them aloft as examples to the old and as inspirations to the young.

In all of scripture the expression, "successful man," appears only once. Joseph is referred to in the Bible as *"Ish matzliach,"* a successful man.[6] The commentators trace the word *matzliach* to a root which means to rise or to vault. That, then, is the true meaning of success—the capacity to rise. It is not merely to advance but to ascend, not merely to go forward but to scale upward. Success is determined not by how far you get, but by how high you reach.

How much, then, is a man worth? It is not the wages that he makes or the compensation he receives. It is not the fortune that he has or the affluence that he enjoys. It is what a person *is;* the life he leads, the ideals he lives by, the goals he sets, the heights he reaches. The estimate of a man's worth—his rating as a man—cannot be obtained from a human credit agency. It comes from a different source. There is a divine standard of value.

6. Gen. 39:2.

5 &

Criteria of Progress

A pilot is reported to have made this announcement to his anxious passengers: "We are off course, but we are making excellent speed."

Whether this incident is true or apocryphal does not really matter. It does, however, illustrate one common notion about progress. So many do regard movement as synonymous with progress and speed as equivalent with advancement.

We had better correct this notion, especially for our generation. For these are fast times in which we live. We relay messages and images from the furthermost vastnesses of outer space with the speed of lightning. We produce every variety of goods at rates that stagger the imagination.

Eight million passenger cars rolled off the assembly lines of the automotive industry of our country last year. Other products and commodities reached the consumer in similar quantity and at parallel rates of production. Speed and quantity have become the principal dimensions of our life.

We are, indeed, like the pilot of our story, making excellent speed. But do we have the assurance that we are not off course? Is human progress to be measured by a speedometer or is it to be regulated by a compass?

The ancient psalmist provided a superb insight for our

problem. "O, Lord," he prayed, ". . . make thy way straight
before me." [1] He, too, wanted desperately to progress. But he
prayed not for speed, but for direction—". . . make thy way
straight for me," he said.

Well, then, if direction is the criterion of progress, how
shall we describe our own age? We have gone far beyond all
former ages in many ways. We enjoy standards of living, opportunities for education, and blessings of freedom and democracy never before known to any society. Judged objec-
tively, we may well regard ours as the age of progress.

Yet there appeared a book recently, entitled "The Age of
Anxiety." In it the author describes not the dark ages, nor the
prehistoric ages, but the twentieth century and our own contemporary times. Is it possible that we have merely advanced
without making progress? "O, Lord, make thy way straight
before me."

Listen to the verdict of Professor Phillip Lee Ralph, not a
clergyman, but a teacher of history. In his book, "The Story
of Our Civilization," he concludes: "At the bottom the trouble with contemporary civilization is that it is immoral." The
author concedes that we have done much to improve the
human condition. He does not deny the advantages that are
ours. But when he surveys the large social environment, his
inevitable conclusion is that "at bottom our civilization is
immoral."

And another historian, Marshall Fishwick, reaches a similar
conclusion.[2] He sees the turmoil of our day and the confusion
of our times. He realizes that the condition is global in character, that it involves the whole human race, two-thirds of
which is colored. He describes our malaise in the language of
the Angel Gabriel in Marc Connelly's "Green Pastures." Recall that Gabriel looked down on our world and said: "Everything nailed down is coming loose."

1. Psalms 5:9.
2. See his Keese Lecture before the University of Chattanooga, as reported
   in the Saturday Review, June 29, 1963.

Here then is the anomaly of our day. It is an Age of Progress, and simultaneously it is an Age of Anxiety. Something is radically wrong. Intrepid astronauts are orbiting the earth for eight successive days, and the inhabitants of that earth are quaking under the threat of nuclear war. Part of the world is suffering from obesity, and the greater part is suffering from malnutrition. Affluence and alcoholism! Crowded campuses and ugly beatniks!

The anomaly is even more mystifying. There are more than forty million students in the schools of our land. Progress! Two million and six hundred thousand crimes were committed in the United States last year [3]—five every minute of the day. Anxiety! Billions in foreign aid—progress! Vietnam —anxiety! A United Nations with one hundred and twenty-seven member-states in it—progress! Red China poised on the borders of India—anxiety. The right to vote at long last granted to every American—progress! Violence in Los Angeles—anxiety!

Thus does the needle on the compass of human destiny fluctuate between anxiety and progress and back again. "O, Lord, make thy way straight before me."

An important criterion of progress now becomes apparent. Progress is never one-dimensional; it is multi-dimensional. The achievement of a single goal in a particular area of life to the exclusion of other important goals is not true progress. There is a spiritual dimension to progress which, if missing, nullifies every advance made. In other words, progress is not merely a movement forward; it is also a movement upward.

A few illustrations may make our thought clearer and more relevant. We did say that eight million cars were produced last year in our country. Let us not forget, however, that one auto is stolen every minute of the day. One-dimensional progress! Forward but not upward.

3. F.B.I. Report, as reported in Herald Tribune, European Edition, July 26, 1965.

We are proud of our nation's abundance. Yet our Secretary of Agriculture is alerting us to what he calls "the crisis of abundance." And do you know why? Because we spend one million dollars a day simply to store our huge surplus food while most of the world's people go to bed hungry every night. One-dimensional progress!

Is it hard to see why there is turmoil in the world? Is it not obvious why our globe is a seething cauldron of hate and envy which recurrently boils over in war and violence and bloodshed? The Food for Peace Program of America is more the symbol of progress—and security—than all the stockpiles of nuclear weapons about which we boast. No, progress is not merely moving forward; it must be a movement upward.

What is true of society and nations is true of individuals. When a man has achieved material success, it may well be said of him that he has made progress—certainly economic progress. But has that success colored the whole spectrum of his life? Listen to William Faulkner, one of our great Nobel laureates:

> "... *perhaps one of the things wrong with our country is success. That there is too much success in it. Success is too easy. In our country a young man can gain it with no more than a little industry. He can gain it so quickly and easily that he has not had time to learn the humility to handle it with, or even to discover that he will need humility.*" [4]

Success without humility, success and mounting divorces; success and estranged children; success and delinquency, among the rich, not the poor; success and marijuana parties on Long Island estates, not in Harlem hovels. Are we ready to label such success as progress? To be sure, those who achieved it did move forward. But did they also move upward?

4. National Book Award Address.

Let us turn to Scripture for guidance on this subject. The central character of Rosh Hashanah is Abraham and his family. It is around him and his household that our Bible reading revolves. What can his life story tell us that will shed light on the problem that engages our attention?

Abraham was the first Bible personality whom God virtually commanded to advance, to progress. "Get thee out of thy country from thy kindred and from thy father's house . . ." [5]

One can almost hear in those holy accents the divine voice saying: "Move Abraham. Get out of Mesopotamia with its pagan cults. You can be more than a foreman in your father's idol shop. The whole world is before you. Go forth and capture it."

And Abraham obeyed. And he became "very rich in cattle and silver and gold." It wasn't long before the small-town boy from Ur became a wealthy Middle East potentate. Did he stop at that? Was material success the terminus of his progress?

Let us read on in that fascinating story of the first Jew. Wheresoever he came, we are told: "And he called in the name of the Lord." [6] And wheresoever he pitched his tent, he established an oasis of hospitality. He brought faith in God to a pagan world and human kindness to those who hungered for it.

And when a moment of crisis arose and two cities were marked for destruction, this successful merchant, this tycoon cattle rancher stood up to God himself. "Wilt thou destroy the righteous with the wicked? . . . Shall not the Judge of all the earth be just?" [7]

Let us read on still further. At a certain stage in his life his concern took a personal turn. "What," said he to God, "canst Thou give me, when I go childless?" [8] He wanted more than

5. Gen. 12:1.
6. Gen. 13:4.
7. Gen. 18:26.
8. Gen. 15:2.

an offspring. He was not satisfied with merely a beneficiary. He wanted an heir—a child of the spirit. He wanted a happy household in which parent and child are bound by the ties of love, understanding and respect.

Only by achieving all this—material success, ethical excellence, family solidarity—could Abraham stand forth as the first and foremost progressive personality in the national gallery of our people.

And the Bible's verdict is precise. "And the Lord blessed Abraham in all things." [9] In *all* things! Progress is only partial when the spiritual dimension is missing. When it is present, progress is true and total.

We may now recognize a further criterion of progress. It is never optional. It is compulsive. It is not left to choice. It is a law of life. If the world will not move forward, then it will be pushed forward.

In nature there is a law of growth. In violation of every law of gravity, the tree will shoot upward toward the sun. Over every blade of grass, says a Jewish mystic, stands an angel who commands it to grow.[10] Life will not surrender to inertia.

> *"From lower to higher next,*
> *Not to the top, is nature's text."*

The same principle operates in man and in his society. Man is called a *holech*—one who moves and advances. He is a creature with built-in progress. He was not meant to stand still. When God commanded Abraham to go forth, our sages explain that he was nudged, pushed forward.[11] It was a case of the divine propulsion of man. Man's destiny is to progress.

It is equally true of society. From the stone age to the nu-

9. Gen. 24:1.
10. Gen. R. 10:7.
11. Midrash Hagadol; Lech.

clear age is the inexorable odyssey of man. Human progress was not continuous, but it was persistent. There were retreats and detours, setbacks and regressions. The graph of human advancement was never a straight line. It was a curve with peaks and depressions, but the trend was ever upward. "A single breaker may recede; but the tide is eventually coming in," is the way Macauley put it.

"Tell the people of Israel to move ahead," [12] was God's command. There will be no return to Egypt. Forty years in a desert, rebellions, defeats, thirst, starvation—all of that must be encountered. But move forward, for in the end is the Promised Land.

That is the fate of civilization. The path of progress is strewn with corpses and stained with blood. And individual progress is no different. There are frustrations and disappointments, defeats and disillusionment. It is easier to go forward than to climb upward. Yet the moral itinerary insists that in the upward direction is true progress. "O, Lord, make thy way straight before me."

A final thought must be spoken. The motivating power behind progress is faith—a great and abiding faith. Without such a faith—in a word, without God—neither man nor his world can move forward. "You cannot ascend, for God is not amongst you," [13] said Moses to a straying and bewildered people.

In every crisis of civilization, when mankind seemed hopelessly mired down in the swamps of inertia, a divine call, a heavenly impulse or a holy slogan provided the motive power to propel it forward.

"Proclaim liberty throughout the land to all the inhabitants thereof." Oh, how much power that generated and how many liberty bells in history began to toll because of it.

"Nation shall not lift up sword against nation, neither shall

12. Exodus 14:15.
13. Num. 14:42.

they learn war any more." My, what an incentive for universal peace this has been and can still continue to be.

"Love thy neighbor as thyself . . . One law and one statute for the stranger and native alike . . . Let all people each walk in the name of his God, and we will walk in the name of the Lord, our God . . ." These are not mere words; they served as the spiritual dynamos to lead men out of the jungle and onto the highways of progress.

How then can we sum up our thought. Progress as a human enterprise must have a spiritual dimension.

Progress, though dependent upon human determination, is in truth a law of life and the second nature of man.

Man cannot advance and leave God behind. For man's will propels him forward, but God's power leads him upward.

6 ❧

A Jewish Insight Into Sin

For the entire day of Yom Kippur our concern will be with sin. We will confess our sins. We will promise to make atonement for them. And we will pray that they be forgiven.

If we are so preoccupied with sin, then we ought to try to understand it better. Job's anxious plea might well be in many a heart this night: "Let me know my sin and my transgression." [1] For to know sin and to understand it is also to learn how to avoid it.

There was a time when sin was the exclusive specialty of religion. Within the temples of religion, sins were confessed. At the altars of religion, sacrifices were brought to atone for sins. From the pulpits of religion, sins were denounced. And the evangelists of many religions dramatically described the fate of "sinners in the hands of an angry God."

In time man became more interested in Man. The social and behavioral sciences came into being, and they began to concern themselves with sin.

The economist searched for the cause of sin in the economic structure of society. He detected a correlation between want and sin, between exploitation and sin, between an unjust economic order and sin.

1. Job 13:23.

The findings of the economist cannot be ignored. It is true, as Scripture wrote, that "man does not live by bread alone." It is equally true, however, and this, too, Scripture wrote, that "let them not despise the thief, if he steal to satisfy himself when he is hungry." [2] The materially underprivileged are easy victims of sin. Yes, and so are the materially overprivileged.

This is, indeed, one of the dilemmas of our times. Half of mankind is counting calories and half is counting pennies. The world seems to be divided between those who suffer from malnutrition and those who struggle against obesity, those who are dieting and those who are hungry. Let us concede to the economist that the underfed and the overfed are ready prey for every sort of devil.

The sociologist, too, became interested in sin. He sought the roots of sin in the social order. He tracked down delinquency to the slums. He studied the relationship between crime and broken homes. He stalked the peddler of narcotics to the hovels of the disillusioned poor and to the mansions of the bored rich. He concluded, therefore, that sin is primarily a product of the social environment.

Let us not ignore the conclusions of the sociologist. Moral climate *is* greatly conditioned by the social environment. Bad housing, inferior education, discrimination in employment, segregation of minorities, crooked politics, dishonesty in high places, cynicism in government, hypocrisy in international affairs—these, of course, are wicked sins in themselves. But they are also infectious germs and deadly viruses that pollute the air and contaminate the atmosphere and spread moral disease over the face of the earth. We had better take to heart the opinions of the sociologist.

The psychiatrist is, of course, interested in sin. More than anyone else he sees the havoc wrought to human personality

2. Prov. 6:30.

by every manner of guilt consciousness. He probes in the dark chambers of the subconscious and discovers there the emotional forces that motivate human conduct and misconduct. He finds that insecurity can beget aggression, that the hunger for love, no less than the hunger for food, can drive a person to evil. He learns that theft is sometimes kleptomania and that alcoholism may be a means of escape from reality. Sin to the psychiatrist is an abnormal compensation for a maladjusted personality. "Man does not sin," said the rabbis of old, "unless he be in a mood of disturbance." [3] Psychiatry confirmed this ancient judgment.

We should be grateful to these sciences—economics, sociology, psychology—for their concern with the problem of sin. Religion should regard them as useful allies in the common effort to reduce evil in the world. More than one head is needed to beat the devil.

Judaism is especially hospitable to any theory that will shed new light on the riddle which is man. This enlightened attitude is the result of the special insights of the Jewish tradition on the problem of sin. What are some of these insights?

First, Judaism maintains that sin is not a congenital condition. It is not inherited; it is acquired. Sinners are not born sinners; they are made.

Many religions hold otherwise. Their theology on this subject runs something like this: Adam, the first man, could have been a perfect creature and could have bestowed perfection upon all his descendants. But—a very big but indeed—he chose to disobey God's command. His disobedience, which in theological parlance is referred to as the Fall of Man, brought upon him and upon all men after him the punishment of God, in the form of "death, suffering, ignorance and a strong inclination to sin." Every human being, therefore, is born with

3. Sota 3a.

the stigma of Original Sin upon him. His mystic blemish can, of course, be washed away by the holy waters of baptism, but the effects of Original Sin abide forever. Man can never shed his predisposition to transgress and to violate the laws of life, of nature and of God.

Except for minor dissents, the overwhelming body of Jewish tradition rejected this view *in toto*. It is contrary to the whole philosophy of Judaism on man and his destiny in the world.

Man, according to Jewish teaching, is born without taint or stigma. At birth he is a *tabula rasa,* a clean slate. Upon that slate he may write a heroic epic of grandeur and righteousness or a sad chronicle of evil and wickedness.

How beautiful are the statements of the Talmud on this subject. "Blessed art thou in thy coming and blessed art thou in thy going—even as you entered this world without sin, so you may depart from it without sin." [4] Sinless at birth, may you be sinless at death.

And here is another: "The Lord loveth the righteous, because their righteousness is not inherited, nor is it due to family position . . . Any man, even a non-Jew, if he desires to be righteous, can be so . . ." [5] Righteousness is not transmitted through genes, and evil is not a matter of genetics. Children may inherit a father's wealth, a mother's good looks or a family business. But righteousness or wickedness are never part of the inherited estate.[6] We had better stop blaming our grandmothers for our moral deficiencies. Morally, we are what we are because we want to be that way. The Original Sin that plagues us is the sin that originates with us.

There now follows a second Jewish insight. Sin is a sickness and the sinner, therefore, is not an evil person but a sick one.

4. Baba Mezia 107a.
5. M.R. Numbers 8:2.
6. Nida 16b.

This diagnosis of sin can be found throughout the religious literature of the Jew.

"O, heal my soul for I have sinned unto you," [7] pleaded David in his Psalms. What he tried to say was: I come to you not for absolution but for adjustment; not for confession but for analysis; not for forgiveness but for a cure.

Some three centuries after David, the great prophet Hosea continued the theme of the Psalmist. "I shall heal their sinfulness," [8] he says in the name of God. Man is not evil; he is ill. He requires not punishment but therapy.

Seventeen centuries later Maimonides crystallized this attitude towards sin and the sinner, recorded it in his famous Code and thus made it the official view of Judaism. That legalist, philosopher and physician supreme refers to sinners, not in theological or moralistic terms, but in medical terms. He considers sinners as "ill with a malady of the soul." [9] He describes the symptoms and prescribes moral medication. Modern psychiatry may disagree with his technique, but it will respect his insight.

This attitude has an important implication. In Judaism the sinner is not despised or abandoned, but pitied and helped. Our faith does not doom him to eternal perdition. It does not sentence him to an interminable purgatory, nor does it hurl him into a bottomless hell. It does not threaten him with extradition into the hands of an angry God. Dante's Inferno is not a Jewish institution; it is definitely restricted. "I desire not the death of the wicked but that the wicked turn from this way and live." [10] The wicked must be nursed back to moral health.

There is a verse in the Psalms which reads, "Let the sinners disappear from the earth and let the wicked be no more." [11] A

7. Psalms 41:5.
8. Hosea 14:5.
9. Maimon. Deoth, Ch. 2: 1 et seq.
10. Ezek. 38.
11. Psalms 104:35.

sage in the Talmud thought that this verse should be understood literally: To hell with the sinners; let them be deported
to where they belong! He was corrected and rebuked. The
proper reading was: "Let *sins*, not the sinners, disappear from
the earth . . ." [12]

Judaism knows of no heretic hunting. Our history has no
record of crusades against sinners or infidels. We never set up
religious inquisitions. There were no torture chambers, third-
degree confessions or forced conversions in Judaism. The notion of "saving souls" is strange to us. We preferred to heal
them. "O heal my soul for I have sinned unto you."

If sin is a disease and the sinner its victim, then we may turn
again to Judaism for a further insight—a most comforting
one, indeed. The disease is curable. The prognosis for the victim is excellent. Complete recovery is possible. The magic
word is—Penitence.

The hardened sinner, the calloused transgressor, the
chronic evildoer—all may look forward optimistically to the
restorative consequences of penitence. "Though your sins be
as scarlet, they shall become white as snow; though they be
red like crimson, they shall be as blanched wool." There is
hope for the sinner. "I will heal their sinfulness," is the divine
assurance; "I will love them freely," [13] is the divine promise.
"Return unto me," is the divine plea, "and I will return unto
you," [14] is the divine pledge. Judaism does not recognize a
"Point of No Return." The gates of penitence are never
shut.[15]

It is much easier to sin than to repent, even as it is easier to
get sick than to get well. How does one repent?

Out of the total Jewish tradition Maimonides distilled three

12. Ber. 10a.
13. Hosea 14:5.
14. Mal. 3:7.
15. M.R. Deut. 2, 7.

principles. They are the three stages in the process of repentance.

The first and the most difficult stage he calls "recognition of the sin." The medical equivalent would be diagnosis, and the theological equivalent would be confession.

It is not easy for an individual to recognize and to admit his error. Psychiatrists know the limits to which people go in order to conceal an evil act. What neurotic muck and dirt must be cleared away before the festering focus of infection is exposed. Yet, not until it is exposed can the healing process begin. It is a great day in the sinner's life when, without fear and without shame, he can beat his breast and say, humbly and remorsefully, "I have sinned."

The second stage in the process of repentance Maimonides calls "regret." This stage is not difficult at all. For regret means relief—relief from the unimaginable torture and torment of guilt-consciousness. Only he who has seen and shared the agony of guilt-laden souls can understand that. If "recognition of the sin" is the exposure of the wound, then "regret" marks the beginning of the healing process.

The third stage is "resolution to sin no more." When one has reached this stage, he has achieved his cure. When, in the language of the liturgy, he is able to say, "O, may it be thy will, O Lord my God and God of my fathers, that I may sin no more . . . ," he is fully recovered—a man at peace with himself, at home in the world and at-one-ment with his God.

How does this process of penitence take place? To whom shall one confess his sin? Before whom shall he admit his regret? To whom shall he make promise to sin no more? Here again Judaism has its own and unique method.

Our faith provides no confessional chamber. There is no religious functionary before whom alone one must open his heart. There is no ecclesiastical authority to grant absolution.

There is no intermediary between man and God. Every man can approach God without an escort—and without an appointment. "Great, indeed, is repentance," say our sages, "for it reaches the very throne of glory." [16] No "pull" is required; no special agent is needed; no fee is necessary. Man all by himself, in his spiritual nakedness, approaches God, all by *himself*,[17] admits his error, expresses his regret, promises to change, and thus receives his forgiveness.

Here is a touching rabbinic legend to illustrate this thought:

There once was a wicked king in Israel. His name was Menashe, son of Hezekiah. He filled God's temple with idols. He brought corruption into the land. He was guilty of every crime, including the murder of the prophet Isaiah. Never would there be forgiveness for him. All the hosts of heaven were determined not to permit his prayers to reach God. What did God do? He built a private tunnel to permit the penitential prayers of Menashe to reach him.[18] Man needs no intermediary. He can even bypass every roadblock that obstructs his way to God. "Thou givest thy hand to sinners, and thy right hand is extended to receive the penitent."

One final thought needs to be spoken. The resolution to depart from sin is easily followed by the decision to pursue righteousness. Repentance requires exertion; rectitude then follows naturally. A quaint Hassidic story will illustrate this thought:

A rabbi was expounding to his disciples a verse from the Psalms. "As far as the East is from the West, so far has he removed our transgressions from us." [19] How far is East from West?" he asked. One disciple answered—from one end of the world to the opposite end. Another replied—from one

16. Yoma 86a.
17. Yalkut, Shim. Hosea.
18. Sanhed. 103a.
19. Psalms 103:12.

point of the horizon to the opposite point. A third suggested —from the rear of the synagogue to the front of it.

The rabbi was not pleased. "Do you know, my children, how far East is from West? Just one turn. Face East, and then make one turn, and you will be facing West."

Are you a three-day-a-year Jew and would like to become a constant Jew? One turn! Are you indifferent to religious observances and would prefer a more positive attitude? One turn! Have you always felt that "charity begins at home," but now recognize obligations to your fellow man? One turn! Have you been squeamish about your Jewish identity and now you choose to be more assertive and proud of your heritage? One turn! Have you thought of Israel as a foreign state underserving of your interest or support, but now you would acknowledge it as a prayer answered and as a dream come true? One turn!

You have been a neglectful husband. Well—one turn! You have been a selfish wife. So—one turn! You frowned upon the "old" generation, old traditions, time-tested ideals, eternal values. Indeed—one turn! From repentance to rectitude—one turn!

Perhaps our entire thought can be summed up in a prayer. O my God, "the soul which thou gavest me was clean." Sin afflicted it and it became sore. "Heal my soul" and cure my sinfulness. Extend thy right hand to receive me. "Turn my heart unto thy testimony." Merciful God, turn me around.

7 ❦

A Religious Analysis of Time

Some years ago Warden Lawes wrote a book to which he gave a strange title, "Twenty Thousand Years in Sing Sing." The author might have been interested merely in choosing a catchy title. Unintentionally, however, he suggested an important thought, that "doing time" is not using time. A "lifer" is not one who makes a life for himself.

Yet, as one observes human behavior he gets the feeling that there are so many outside of prison walls who seem to be "doing time;" serving out, as it were, a life sentence. The Psalmist speaks of such as these:

> "The days of our years are three score and ten,
> And if by reason of strength,
> They be four score years,
> Yet is their pride but travail and nothingness,
> For it is soon gone by and we fly away."

This melancholy mood, sooner or later, descends upon all of us. As the gears of time grind away relentlessly, eating up the years, consuming the decades, we become terrified by our own brevity and crushed by the utter futility of it all. Out of the depths of existential despair, we cry out with Tennyson:

> *"Let us alone. Time driveth onward fast,*
> *And in a little while our lips are dumb.*
> *Let us alone. What is it that will last?*
> *All things are taken from us and become*
> *Portions and parcels of the dreadful past."*

This mood hits us hardest when we begin to feel that time is running out, that it is later than we think.

It hits the worker whose life was a boring routine—eight hours a day, forty hours a week, fifty weeks a year for all the weeks that he can remember—who suddenly wonders: where have the years vanished and what have I done with them. He realizes *what the years have done with him,* but he cannot explain what *he has done with the years.* Poor creature, he was not aware that he was merely "doing time."

It hits the prosperous businessman, the affluent industrialist, the successful executive. After building huge industrial empires and pyramiding corporations upon corporations, it dawns upon these paragons of success that they have been in error all their life. They thought all along that they were running their businesses, only to discover that their businesses had been running them. The evidence of that discovery is frequently shattering. Health becomes impaired, and its symptoms are, alas, universal—strange pains across the chest, a tiredness that is not relieved by rest, a physician's caution to take it easy, and sometimes even forced membership in the all too rapidly growing fraternity of coronary thrombosis.

It is then that reflection starts and remorse sets in. One begins to realize how desperately children needed a father all through the years and how much they still need him; how genuinely a wife longed for her husband, but was denied his companionship and love; how frantically a community, an institution, a people, could have used a gifted potential leader who unfortunately was too busy to care.

Well, are the "lifers" limited to penal institutions? Are

there not many spinning out their existence in the manner of serving a sentence? How many are *using time* and how many more are "doing time?"

The problem of learning how to use time must have troubled even so supreme a personality as Moses. It was out of a deep emotional as well as practical necessity that he appealed to God: "Teach us to number our days that we may get us a heart of wisdom." [1]

No man had greater need for time. A horde of slaves had to be emancipated and then transformed into a people. A divine faith had to be imparted to that people, and through it to all mankind. A rebellious mob had to be transported through a perilous wilderness. And beyond, there was a Promised Land that had to be conquered. What a busy life for one man! No wonder that, prompted by practical necessity, Moses prayed: "Teach us to number our days that we may get us a heart of wisdom."

But that prayer was also induced by emotional necessity. Here was a man confronted by what Plato called, "the image of eternity," grappling with the profoundest mystery of life —time. Listen to him as he tries to comprehend that mystery. "O Lord, thou hast been a dwelling place unto us in all generations . . . For a thousand years in thy sight are but as yesterday when it is past and as a watch in the night . . . The days of our years are three score and ten, or even by reason of strength, four score years; yet is their pride but travail and nothingness; for it is soon gone by and we fly away."

Here is man, the finite, standing before God, the infinite. Here is a time-bound creature contemplating the Divine who is timeless. He sees year succeeding year in relentless progression. He knows that before long the blood of youth will fade and physical power will diminish. Presently furrows will ap-

1. Psalms 90:12.

pear on a once smooth countenance and wrinkles will etch themselves into an erstwhile fresh complexion. No one is particularly happy at the flight of the years or about the prospects of old age. So Moses, in a melancholy mood and out of deep anguish, prayed, and each of us echoes that prayer: "Teach us to number our days that we may get us a heart of wisdom."

What, then, can we say to ourselves, as time-bound creatures, that will enable us to live courageously and productively? What attitude shall we adopt towards time—not time as a mathematical dimension or as a metaphysical abstraction, but time as a commodity, as a public and private utility?

The first thing for us to realize is that while God is the author of time, man is its master. He makes the calendar; he composes the almanac. Speak, if you will, about the sands of time; it is man, however, who makes the footprints in them.

Our Rabbis expressed that thought in their usual poetic manner.[2] The angels inquire of God, "When will the New Year begin?" And God responds, "Do not ask that of me; you and I will address that inquiry to the Court below."

How true! It is not God but man who decides when a new year will begin. It is man who determines when a fresh era of hope will dawn upon the world. It is man who proclaims the inauguration of a promising century of progress. Long stretches of prosperity and prolonged periods of depression; dark ages of bigotry and endless centuries of enlightenment; brutal eras of war and bloodshed, and bright epochs of peace and security—all these are manifestations of time. They are, however, the product of man's doing and the results of his efforts or failures.

It is man who can swing forward or backward the hands of the clock of history. In the mad game of life, when the com-

2. Cant. R. 5:5.

petitive spirit runs so high that men and nations are at each other's throats and threaten to demolish the world and to exterminate the human race, it is man who can then exclaim: Time out! Stop this madness! And if man truly wills it, he can stop it. Yes, indeed, God is the author of time, but man is the timekeeper.

If we realize that man is the master of time, then we will stop the use of certain loose and whimsical expressions. We will, for example, never say: Don't worry; time will take care of everything. What an erroneous attitude that is. Imagine if parents were to adopt that attitude when a child is born. From infancy to maturity, do they allow time to take care of him? Parents know the labor, the love, the sacrifice, the pain, and the tears that go into the development of a child. No, time does not take care of everything. We do.

Does time heal sorrow and cure grief? Those of us who deal with people in bereavement know that there are some wounds that will never mend and some afflictions for which there is no consolation. What we try to do is to help people discover reservoirs of faith and strength within themselves and to tap these reservoirs, so that they may restore drooping spirits and revive wilted souls. No, time does not take care of sorrow. We do.

Did time take care of everything in 1939 when aggression was on the march and tyranny rampant? To be sure, there were some who were prepared to leave it to time. They counselled a short-sighted policy of muddling through, of "peace in our time," with little worry as to what may come after us. But fortunately there were those who, like Joshua of old, commanded time to stand still until the enemies of mankind were brought to their knees. No, we did not allow time to take care of everything. We did.

We should now recognize that if man is the master of time, then he must act like one. Time requires regulation and man must be the one to regulate it. Inevitably the statement of Ecclesiastes floats up to the foreground of our memory.[3] "To everything there is a season, and a time for every purpose under the heaven." Oh, how one wishes that we would take such counsel to heart.

"There is a time to plant and a time to uproot"—this was not meant only for farmers.

"A time to weep and a time to laugh"—how often we cry at the wrong time and laugh when we should be crying?

"A time to mourn (or to be serious) and a time to dance" —tell this to our playful sons and daughters who think they can jitterbug their way through life.

"A time to embrace and a time to refrain from embracing" —let parents who either smother their children with love or deprive them of it learn this lesson.

"A time to be silent and a time to speak"—let our prattlers and gossipers take heed of that.

"A time of war and a time of peace"—my, how many statesmen can profit from that!

We are so proficient in organizing administrative calendars, work schedules and time sheets. Would that we could learn to do the same for our lives.

If we learned that, we would rarely be confronted by the individual who, though important in his own eyes and admired by others, is nonetheless a pathetic character. I refer to the individual with a *crowded* life.

Dr. Harry Emerson Fosdick refers somewhere to a sign outside of a theatre or a concert hall which invariably makes him sad. It reads: "Standing Room Only." Yet how many people carry such signs around with them all the time. A great

3. Eccl. 3:1.

cause in need of workers appeals to them. But the auditorium of their life is already full. For that great cause there is "Standing Room Only." A great book needs to be read. But, alas, there is no time for it: "Standing Room Only!" A wife is craving for love and companionship. Children are seeking the understanding and guidance of a father. A home is desolate without the steadying and directing hand of a parent. But, alas, life is crowded. "Standing Room Only" for all these. *Crowded* lives, indeed, but not full lives.

That is what Moses meant when he prayed as all of us must pray: "Teach us to number our days that we may get us a heart of wisdom."

Our discussion should now make us realize that it has an important bearing upon the problem of the age of man. Every one of us really has two ages, the chronological or quantitative age, and the achievement or qualitative age.

There is an intimation of that in Scripture. The Bible records that when Jacob came to Egypt, Pharaoh asked him, "How old art thou?" [4] Those that are familiar with the answer will recall that it was rather involved and complicated. Said Jacob: "The years of my sojournment are one hundred and thirty; few and evil were the days of my life; and they did not reach the years of life of my fathers in the days of their sojournment."

Oh, Jacob, the man asked you a simple question. Why don't you give him a simple answer? The truth is that the question, "How old are you?," is never a simple one. Says Marcel Proust, "Those who count by days and by years are fools. Days are perhaps equal for a clock, but not for a man."

By chronological standards, Keats was twenty-six when the song of his life was silenced. But when you read "Ode to a Nightingale" or "Endymion," you sense a mature heart and a

4. Gen. 47:8, 9.

ripened soul. Mozart was thirty-seven when his musical genius was snapped by death. But when you hear his concertos, you know that all that majestic melody was, to use a rabbinic metaphor, "old wine pouring forth from a new flask." The Biblical Joseph was thirty when he reconstructed the entire economy of an ancient empire, and a grateful people bowed before his chariot and exclaimed, "young in years but old in wisdom."

You were right, Father Jacob; it is not easy to answer the question, "How old art thou?" "Time," says Shakespeare in "As You Like It," "travels in divers paces with divers persons. I will tell you who time ambles withal, who time trots withal, who time gallops withal, and who time stands still withal."

See how important is the prayer: "Teach us to number our days that we may get us a heart of wisdom."

We are now prepared to recognize that there is a dimension of time that is all too frequently overlooked. *Time is holy!* Hours, months, years, light-years, these are but prosaic categories. Sunrises, sunsets, seasons are but the visible undulations of time. Clocks, speedometers, stop watches are merely the arbitrary measurements of time. Above and beyond all these is the dimension of the holiness of time.

Time is a mathematical category, says the scientist. Time is money, says the businessman. Time is holy, says Judaism. In our tradition we sanctify the month—*kiddush ha-hodesh*. We sanctify the seventh day—*shabbat kodesh*. A festival is called *mikra kodesh*, a holy convocation. The penitential period is called the High Holy Day season. Every time a Jew raises a cup of wine to consecrate a festival, he asserts that God "sanctifies Israel and the seasons."

How is time sanctified? Our tradition teaches us that too. Sabbaths, holidays, festivals, we are instructed, should be divided into two equal parts: half for man's personal needs, pleasures and enjoyment, and half for the service of God.[5] To a lesser extent that ought to apply to every day of our life. Let us slice off a portion of the day for rest, for constructive leisure, for intellectual recreation, for human service, for assistance to our fellow man, for the improvement of society. Even as there is imposed upon us an income tax, so ought we to impose upon ourselves a *time tax,* to compel us to contribute a portion of our time for holy purposes.

Some years ago there was a popular song which had a significant line. It ran like this: "My time is your time." A lyricist had a great intuition. "In thy hand is my time," says the Psalmist. This is the very thought that should be impressed upon us: that our time should at least partly be His time.

In the war just ended, before embarking upon an important mission, the pilots of a squadron would be assembled to be briefed on all the phases of their mission. Finally, the squadron commander would say, "Gentlemen, synchronize your watches."

Above us all, sending us forth upon our mission in life, with all its hazards and distractions, there stands the Supreme Commander of the Universe, with the clock of eternity in His hand, and He says: "My children, synchronize your watches."

O, Lord, "Teach us to number our days that we may get us a heart of wisdom."

5. Beza 15b.

Part II

The Practical Uses of Faith

8 ♋

The Practical Uses of Faith

For those with faith there are no questions, and for those without faith there are no answers. The Chofetz Chayim, sainted Rabbi of Radin, is responsible for this simple but profound epigram.

Yet the matter cannot be left just that way. There are times when men of faith do have questions to ask and when those without faith must not go unanswered. This would apply to times like our own.

Rarely, in the whole saga of human history, has a generation more aptly been called a "Crisis Generation." A recent cartoon provided a candid snapshot of our times. It showed a distraught business executive gazing out of the window of a skyscraper office building and despondently saying to himself: "Ah, for the good old days, when we had nothing to fear except fear itself."

Let us take a glimpse at the picture. Six continents and the three billion people who inhabit them, two-thirds of them colored, are seething with hate and heaving with turmoil. Human blood is running thick in many places—in the wild underbrush of erstwhile jungles and in the staid cities of long-established democracies. From behind the bamboo curtain come screams of horror and from behind the iron curtain

63

issue threats of war and destruction. In the language of an old play: "Everything nailed down is coming loose."

At such a time those with faith do have questions and those without faith do require answers. All of us are racked with doubt and are trembling with fright. In the metaphor of Isaiah, we are looking for a faith with which to gird our sagging loins. When the prophet said, "The Lord is my strength and my fortress, and my refuge in the day of afflic- tion," [1] he must have been speaking to us—to our tired and troubled generation. Oh, how badly we need a sturdy and practical faith.

Let us take another glimpse at the picture. At least two hundred and seventy-five thousand persons are expected to die of cancer in the United States this year. There are two and a half million mentally retarded children in the United States today. One hundred and twenty-six thousand such children are born every year in our country. Ten thousand people die of hunger and malnutrition every day in our "afflu- ent" world. Most of the world's population, it was recently reported, go to bed hungry every night. And simultaneously, fifty million Americans are overweight to the point of ob- esity.

How long can such a condition prevail without shaking the very foundations of our world? To prevent such a universal calamity, we apparently need more than food, more than the visible and tangible things of life. We need what the Psalmist called, "a way of faith"—a practical and sustaining faith. We need the Lord as strength and fortress, and as refuge in the day of affliction.

We had better recognize one thing at once. The infantile and erroneous notions about faith will not do for the cruel, harsh and exacting realities of our day. One of these notions is that faith implies resignation, surrender, passive reliance upon

1. Jer. 16:1.

some supernatural power. Man himself, according to this notion, is a helpless tool in the hands of an inexorable destiny. He is a frail bark, driven to and fro by the angry and relentless currents of life. Salvation may come to him, but he can do nothing to bring it on.

This notion may apply to some religions—not to Judaism. Our tradition stresses not fate but choice. Man is not a driven leaf; he is but "little lower than the angels." He is not a storm-tossed bark; he is the captain of his ship and can steer it into whatever port he wills.

Nor is faith blind credulity, compulsive entanglement in a web of superstition. Judaism long ago cautioned against that. "Be not dismayed by the signs of heaven," [2] taught Jeremiah. Astrology and similar clap-trap is for the weak of mind and sick of soul; not for the strong and proud creature made in God's image.

And of course, faith is not belief in a divine dispenser of tranquilizers and barbiturates. God does not, as it were, stand over man's shoulder, like a caressing father over a trembling child, and patting him on the back, speak to him softly: "Don't worry, old chap; daddy will take care of everything. He will teach you 'the Power of Positive Thinking'; he will give you 'Peace of Mind' and Peace of Soul. Hush, my child, go to sleep now."

This lullaby kind of religion will not do for our day. We need a hard, tough and sturdy faith. "The Lord is my strength . . ." He is power, force and energy. When properly used He provides the fortress and the refuge in the day of affliction.

It is not difficult now to recognize the first positive attribute of a healthy and mature faith. Faith is a capacity which enables man to face the challenge of life. Every

2. Jer. 10:2.

achievement of life is the result of some challenge, and the successful response to that challenge is made possible by faith.

Here is one example: Primitive man encountered darkness. For ages he was mystified by it. He was in constant terror of it. He peopled it with devils and demons. He composed weird incantations to placate the evil spirits which flapped their black wings in the caverns of night.

Then came someone obsessed by a hunch that darkness can be conquered. The hunch became a conviction; the conviction stimulated experimentation; and the experimentation resulted in the invention of light. First came the small flame, then the single candle, and now the spotlight which pierces the heavens with a shaft of thirty thousand candle power. Superstition conceived of night as a monstrous dragon eating up the sun. Faith made possible the flash bulbs popped off by astronauts and satellites that can photograph the earth at a distance of five hundred miles and that are five hundred times brighter than the sun.

See what faith can do! Faith released the genius of man. Then, like the God who endowed him with that genius, man said, "Let there be light; and there was light."

Thus did man confront the many challenges of life. Challenged by nature, he learned to imitate it in art, in poetry and in music. Challenged by distance, he perfected speed. Challenged by the immensity of the universe, he winged his way aloft into the vast stretches of space. Challenged by the mystery of life, he discovered God.

Let us not, however, associate challenge only with scientific discoveries, with inventions of every variety, with art, music, or theology. Life itself is a challenge—the greatest challenge of all. The capacity to live is impossible without the capacity to believe. Life must go together with faith. Otherwise life merely splutters, flickers and is snuffed out.

Here are a few facts to ponder. Close to twenty thousand

people commit suicide in the United States every year. More than half a million are in mental institutions and God knows how many are receiving private treatment. A half million people become alcoholics in the United States every year.[3] There are at least two hundred thousand divorces in America each year and the number is increasing.

And yet, ours is a land of abundance. Most of us have almost everything we want. One out of every three Americans is overweight. We have become Metrecal addicts and our national preoccupation is dieting. What has happened then, that so many cannot meet the challenge of life?

Let a teacher of religion venture a diagnosis of our collective *malaise*. "The disease with which the human mind now labors," said Emerson in his day, "is want of faith." And the Psalmist in his day expressed it after his own fashion: "Help us, O, Lord . . . when faith has vanished from mankind." [4] We have lost faith in ourselves, faith in our fellow-man, faith in our society, faith in the world. And beyond all these, we have lost faith in a Supreme Providence. Yes, we have lost faith in God, and we had better recover that loss ere we lose much more. We cannot do much longer without a God who is strength, fortress and refuge.

But faith offers more than a capacity to meet the challenges of life. It is, in addition, a powerful influence in the formation of moral character. When man turns the dynamics of faith in upon himself, he transforms the whole structure of his moral personality.

A man possessed of faith does more than observe the full regimen of his religion. He not only keeps the Sabbath and festivals, but through them he sanctifies his life. He not only obeys the dietary laws, but they become for him a system of

3. Statistics of the Department of Health, Education and Welfare.
4. Psalms 12:2.

discipline to regulate his appetites and to control his desires. He learns that reverence for God is impossible without respect for man. By recognizing the authority of God, he simultaneously cultivates honor for a father, love for a mother, loyalty for a friend, and duty to society.

Listen to this from a book on mental illness just published by Cornell University: [5] "The next time you go to a normal party of about ten or twelve guests, look around the room carefully. If it is a statistically average group, one of the people there has been, is, or will be, mentally ill during his lifetime and a patient in a mental hospital."

And here is another quote from the same book: "Up to the age of forty-five, suicide is the fourth largest cause of death in the United States."

In the face of such authentic revelations, I must humbly submit that I am not talking psychiatry, nor am I even preaching religion. I am pleading for character—strong, sturdy, healthy character. I am pleading for men and women who can face life courageously and meet death fearlessly; who can encounter difficulty heroically, and suffer disappointments stoically.

I am thinking of young people who will not wilt and collapse under the impact of life's problems; whom adversity will not destroy and whom good fortune will not spoil. I am thinking of young men and young women who will understand the meaning of love and the joy and sacredness of marriage; to whom life is more than indulgence and existence, more than the quest for new thrills and greater pleasures. I am thinking of children who will not only know the cost of *things* but the value of principles; who will receive with gratitude and give with generosity; who will know how to spend but also how to sacrifice.

5. New York City Bar Association and Cornell Law School: Foreword to *Mental Illness and Due Process.*

If faith can contribute to the development of such character, as I believe it can, then I plead for such faith. My, how true are the prophet's words! "The Lord is my strength and my fortress and my refuge in the day of affliction."

But faith does even more. It creates an atmosphere of optimism in which man can live in hope. The man of faith realizes that God cares. He will not abandon the world, nor will He forsake man. His ways are inscrutable; His judgments are hard to understand and even harder to accept. But He cares! Our sacred literature even speaks of God as crying, shedding tears as he slides the shuttle of his will over the loom of life.

God cares—What comfort there is in that! Even the stricken and suffering Job must have felt it when, in agony, he exclaimed,[6] "I know that my Redeemer liveth." God cares! Abraham felt it when he entreated, "Shall not the Judge of all the earth be just?" Moses experienced it when he protested against the divine decision to destroy his people. "And God repented." God cares!

> *"When blessings bring Thy*
> *sunshine to our heart,*
> *Let gratitude uplift each*
> *soul at rest;*
> *And when to bear our*
> *griefs becomes our part,*
> *Let faith and hope exhort*
> *us—God knows best."*

A famous author and historian recently put it well when he said,[7] "Our best weapon against to-day's doubt is human faith. Man has not come this far merely to annihilate himself." From the caveman to modern society is a long road that has

6. Job 19:25.
7. Fishwick, Marshall W.: Keese Lecture at University of Chattanooga. Reported in *Saturday Review*, June 29, 1963.

taken millenia to travel. There were detours and dead ends, blind alleys and dangerous curves. Draw a graph of man's history on this planet and see the peaks and depressions. But notice, too, how the trend is irresistibly forward and upward. Man was counted out so often in the arena of history only to rise again. He is battered but not crushed; beaten but not defeated; at the moment groggy, but still on his feet. The divine referee will continue to hold up the hand of man, the intrepid warrior, and declare to the end of time—"Winner and still champion."

It is remarkable that the word for faith in Hebrew is "Emunah". The same word also has another meaning— steady.[8] Does not that sum up our whole thought? What is Faith if not steadiness? Confronted by the challenges of life, man hears a divine voice which says—"Steady." When character becomes shaky, the same voice says—"Steady, now." When gloom descends and sorrow falls, the voice again says, "Steady, son, steady!"

8. Ex. 17:12.

9 ❧

Overcoming a Sense
of Loneliness

A book with a very significant title was published several years ago. It is an excellent sociological portrait of our society and is called "The Lonely Crowd."

The very title should make us reflect. Our generation is apparently a lonely generation, and twentieth century man is a lonely creature. The sociologist observes it; the psychiatrist is disturbed by it; and the teacher of religion must deal with it. Together they must agree that "it is not good that man should be alone . . ." [1]

On the surface, our generation has no cause for loneliness. A multitude of reasons could be marshalled in support of this contention. Let us examine some of these reasons.

To begin with, statistics seem to refute the notion of loneliness. Numerically the human family is larger than ever before in history. When it was recorded in Genesis that "it is not good that man should be alone," there was only one Adam in the world. Today there are close to three billion people in the world. How can man be lonely among so many of his kind?

How? Because statistics are not society, and "a crowd is not

1. Gen. 2:18.

company and faces are but a gallery of pictures." [2] Indeed, one of the causes of man's loneliness is that he has become merely a number in a table of vital statistics. Made in the image of God, his divine physiognomy is of little importance. He and his fellows have been reduced to curves of distribution on population graphs. A creature intended to be "little short of the angels" senses an existential loneliness as he is stripped of his human identity. "It is not good that man should be alone."

We had reason to expect that the progressive contraction of the world would eliminate the sense of loneliness of modern man. The world has indeed become smaller. New York is nearer to Australia today than it was to Chicago fifty years ago. We are now able to converse with each other, even to see each other, though separated by thousands of miles. The world has become one neighborhood. How can one be lonely in such a world?

How? Because the conquest of space does not imply the eradication of mental barriers, the removal of racial boundaries, the razing of religious barricades and the lifting of iron curtains. Space may have shrunk, but social distance has not. Men are undoubtedly *nearer* to each other, but not *closer*. Just as soon as a continent is brought nearer to another, the threat of an inter-continental missile shatters the prospect of unity. And man trembles once again in his loneliness.

But what of the enormous conveniences that modern man has; the things he possesses; the comforts he enjoys; the luxuries at his disposal? Are they not capable of preventing loneliness?

Let us look to Scripture for an answer. When God said, "It is not good that man should be alone," He did not say it about some primordial creature lying in a sequestered forest or a forsaken marsh. He said it about Adam, who was at that mo-

2. Bacon, Sir Francis: Essays: *Of Friendship.*

ment disporting himself in a luxurious Garden of Eden. However scholars may interpret that Garden of Eden, as real or allegorical, does not matter. There was Adam with a paradise all to himself, lying in the luscious shade, unfettered by garments, untroubled by calories, munching at fruit that was "delightful to behold and good to eat." The verdant beauty about him, the music of brooks and birds, the trees of knowledge and of life were *all* his to enjoy. And it is of that Adam, in the midst of that splendor, that the Bible writes, "It is not good that man should be alone."

> ". . . *In solitude*
> *What happiness; who can enjoy alone,*
> *Or all enjoying, what contentment find?*" [3]

A lonely paradise can be a depressing hell. *Things* never take the place of people. Pleasures are no substitute for companionship. Possession is not fulfillment. Amidst all the abundance of our civilization, its glitter and gaiety, its neon lights and radios, its air conditioning and television, many of us, alas, find ourselves, sullen and lonely, playing—emotionally at least—solitaire.

Oppressed by loneliness, many seek relief and release from its torments. The list of the afflicted is a long one and includes every segment of our society. The "misunderstood" husband and the unloved wife are on it. The rebellious adolescent and the disappointed parent are there. The bored rich and the underprivileged poor are there too. There is a line for those who are "tired of livin' and afraid of dyin'." There are a few aliases on the list: the "problem child," a pseudonym for a problem parent; the "senior citizen," a euphemism for the neglected aged. What a long and melancholy list of lonely hearts!

How valiantly they struggle against their loneliness and, alas, how futile are the efforts. In one year Americans spent

3. Milton: *Paradise Lost.*

some ten billions of dollars on liquor, much of it unquestionably in an attempt to overcome loneliness. Can a highball cure a lonely heart?

In 1957 some eighty-one thousand children were born out of wedlock to teen-age mothers.[4] Unless the situation is controlled, the National Conference of Social Work was recently told, the figure will soon reach one hundred and twenty thousand. Can a moment of clandestine love drive away loneliness?

Well-intentioned friends are always ready with advice, and the desperately lonely follow the advice. Enroll in a Lonely Hearts Club; take up golf; buy yourself a new hat; get him a dog; go off on a cruise—these are some of the suggestions. Can one really escape from loneliness? Can an external remedy heal an internal malady? "It is not good that man should be alone."

There are no palliatives or panaceas by which to overcome loneliness. No miracle drugs are available and no quick cures possible. Nothing short of a radical and basic reorientation to life will achieve results. "And I will give unto you a new heart, and a new spirit will I place within you . . ."[5] The lonely heart must be replaced by a "new heart."

The "new heart" will first and foremost cultivate love. Loneliness can only brood in a cold and empty heart. When love enters, solitude must depart.

Consider the miracle that love wrought for the biblical first man. Adam, according to the rabbinic interpreters, was a weak and helpless specimen. He wandered about in the Garden of Eden aimlessly and forlornly. He feared the shadows and was terrified by the setting sun. All night long he trembled lest the morrow never come and destruction be his fate and the fate of his world.

4. Oettinger, Mrs. Katherine Brownell, Chief, Federal Children's Bureau: *New York Times,* May 29, 1959.
5. Ezekiel 36:26.

Then a helpmate, "suited unto him," was placed at his side. Love entered his life. The scared and lonely Adam was transformed into the courageous and confident father of the race, the biblical progenitor of all mankind. He was no longer alone; there was love at his side.

Love awakened curiosity. He was persuaded to partake of the Tree of Knowledge. The quest for wisdom thereafter became a desirable enterprise. The Tree of Life became a challenge, and the mysteries of existence no longer held terrors. He had banished loneliness. There was love at his side.

God's punishment was severe. "By the sweat of thy brow shalt thou eat bread." Even that did not matter. A caressing hand will wipe away the sweat. The earth will be stubborn; labor will be cruel. That, too, did not matter. The labor will not be in his behalf alone. It will be a labor of love. Thorns and thistles will bruise and hurt "till thou returnest unto the earth from which thou wast taken." Strange, but even death had lost its terror. There was love at his side.

The expulsion from Eden was a shock, a severe traumatic experience. But paradise without love is a wasteland, and a wasteland in which there is love can be paradise. As these two fugitives fled from Eden they were really two lovers on a sight-seeing tour of their destiny.

The old Adam and Eve story which used to fascinate us as children offers new meaning and fresh insight to us as mature men and women. Its message is crisp and concise. Paradise is what it is because love blooms in it. A jungle is what it is because hate and greed are spawned in it. Our world, which can be a paradise, is what it is because we allow it to resemble a jungle

"I remember the grace of thy youth, the love of thy betrothal . . ." [6] Such romance is the key to happy wives and less lonely husbands.

6. Jer. 2:2.

"And his banner over me is love." [7] Homes decorated with such banners cannot be gloomy or lonely.

"And ye shall love the stranger." [8] If nations made that part of their national policy, their citizens would be less sad and sullen.

"Love thy neighbor as thyself." [9] If this were not only pious preachment but practical performance, then our society would not be characterized as "The Lonely Crowd."

> *"Through the wide world he only is alone*
> *Who lives not for another. Come what will*
> *The generous man has his companions still."*

Thus sang the poet. The average person transposed this sentiment into simpler language—"all the world loves a lover." A preacher is tempted to use a slight variation—"every lover loves the world."

In addition to the cultivation of love, the lonely of heart will have to cultivate a second quality. Let us call it a sense of continuity. This involves the recognition that man is the sumtotal of generations. The roots of his personality are sunk deep in the soil of the past. His conduct is the result of accumulated traditions. His soul is the repository of inherited traits. He is in a sense a suspension bridge over which march the legions of the past. In a word, man is more than the product of biology; he is also the product of history.

Ralph Waldo Emerson contributed a graphic metaphor for this thought. Said he, "Every man is an omnibus on which all his ancestors are seated." How can man be lonely when such invisible company is always with him?

Long before Emerson, however, the Jewish tradition provided an even better illustration of this thought. Recall the

7. Song of Songs 2:4.
8. Deut. 10:19.
9. Lev. 19:18.

story of Jacob fleeing from Laban, a not over-kind father-in-law. He was preparing to meet Esau, a brother who bore him an ancient grudge. At one point of this episode the bible tells us: "And Jacob was left alone." [10] Never was a man lonelier than he in the darkness of that crucial night. Danger behind him; uncertainty ahead of him, and an unknown adversary about to assail him! There he stood, a solitary, forlorn, desperate figure, upon the bleak plains of Mesopotamia.

"And Jacob was left alone." The sages of the Talmud read this verse and sensed the plight of that lonely wanderer. Listen to their observation: "And Jacob was left alone"—"alone in a cave with his ancestors." [11] What a commentary on the nature of loneliness! What they tried to say was that Jacob was not really alone. His dear ones were not with him; his kinsmen were not near him; he was perplexed and afraid. But he was not alone. His ancestors were with him. He saw his father Isaac and remembered when, as a child, he kneeled to receive the paternal blessing. He recalled his patriarchal grandfather Abraham and the tales of spiritual heroism that he had heard about him. The image of his mother Rebekah flashed before him, and he felt her tears and her tenderness. No man is alone who has such ancestors to spur him on. No man is alone when he can recall a past of which he is a continuing strand. No man is alone when he can cling to a chain of tradition in which he is the latest link.

A sense of continuity is of particular pertinence to the Jew. Loneliness was our fate from the very beginning of our history. ". . . Behold, it is a people that shall dwell alone . . ." [12] —This was a prediction which, alas, came true. We knew the loneliness of the slave in Egypt. We experienced the solitude of a monotheistic people in a pagan world. For nineteen centuries we were the lonely exiles of the earth. For ages we

10. Gen. 32:25.
11. Midrash Yelamdenu.
12. Num. 23:9.

dwelt in solitary confinement in the ghettos of the world. Within our own day millions of our kin were sealed off in concentration camps and perished in lonely agony in the crematoria of Europe. The descendants of Jacob, like their ancestor, were indeed alone.

Even the contemporary Jew experiences this sense of loneliness. A restricted hotel returns his application for a reservation, and his pride is wounded. An exclusive tennis club rejects a Negro, and a Jewish face blanches with fear. A "Gentleman's Agreement" bars him from setting up home in some area, and he feels unwanted. When well-meaning friends declare that "some of my best friends are Jews," he squirms in self-consciousness. Jacob's loneliness descends upon him.

But need the Jew feel lonely? Within our veins courses the blood of kings and prophets, of sages and singers, of poets and philosophers. Moses is our kinsman; Maimonides is our brother. Even as we commune with our God during this Holy Day Season, so did the philosopher Gabriol nine hundred years ago and Hillel one thousand years before him. What a tradition, what an ancestry! How can one be lonely amidst such company?

Those who reject such company and who abandon such a tradition are exposing themselves to all the torments of loneliness and to all its evil consequences. Let us return a moment to Emerson's metaphor: "Every man is an omnibus on which his ancestors are seated." There is only one type of Jew who can feel lonely—the Jew who misses this omnibus.

There is a third quality that must be cultivated if loneliness is to be overcome—a consciousness of the presence of God. That seems so vague; yet it is so real. It was real to Moses, who in the stillness of the desert heard the voice of the Lord. It was real to David, who in the silence of the night looked up to the starry skies and proclaimed, "The Heavens declare the glory of God." It was real to the Psalmist who, though walking in the valley of the shadow of death, feared no evil, for God was with him. And it will be real to any sensitive person who will keep the slogan of the pietist ever in his heart. "I have set the Lord before me always." [13]

Lonely will be those who under the spell of a mechanistic philosophy will conceive of man as an accident. Lonely will be they who regard the world as a fortuitous occurrence. Lonely will be they who think of life as a mechanical contrivance, whirling in some orbit, guided by no one, bound for nowhere and doomed to ultimate disintegration. Lonely will be those who, with Coleridge's Ancient Mariner, will find themselves

> *"Alone, alone, all all alone*
> *Alone on a wide, wide sea.*
> *So lonely 'twas that God Himself*
> *Scarce seemed there to be."*

But he who senses the presence of God is never at a loss for companionship. In the hushed chamber of illness he hears, "For I, the Lord, am thy healer." [14] In the loneliness of orphanhood he knows that "when my father and my mother leave me, the Lord gathers me in." [15] In sorrow he will have someone to lay him down in green pastures; in distress a steady hand will lead him to still waters. How can man be alone when he is conscious of the ever-presence of God?

No, man need not be alone. Love dispels loneliness. A sense of continuity banishes solitude. God provides companionship.

13. Psalms 16:8.
14. Ex. 15:26.
15. Psalms 27:10.

10

Coping With a Sense of Guilt

A brilliant doctor, a genius in medical research, recently informed the Dean of his medical school that he was going to have surgery done on himself. He explained his own diagnosis —inoperable cancer of the colon.

His diagnosis was later confirmed. For six months he had observed the unmistakable symptoms of the dread disease, but did nothing about it, when something could have been done. He is now in the terminal stages of the disease, waiting in agony for inevitable death.

The brilliant pianist, Kelberin, struggled for years to achieve the cherished ambition of every gifted musician—a performance at Carnegie Hall in New York. He finally did achieve that. His program included the "Totentanz" by Franz Liszt. He played it superbly and was acclaimed by the critics. But he never knew of it. When a friend came to his home to congratulate him, she found a note which read: "After I finish the 'Totentanz,' I will not be alive any more."—Alas, a hapless suicide.

A young industrialist became a tycoon after much effort. He made millions and was on the way to more millions. He was admired and respected as a dramatic symbol of unusual success. One day he lost it all—fortune, position and reputation—in a wild gamble and in a venture that must end in prison.

These instances are from real life. Who knows what is behind them? Why should a scientific genius wait until an operable cancer becomes inoperable? Why should a musical virtuoso snuff out his life as he attains musical fame? Why should a brilliant enterpriser at the pinnacle of financial success plunge into a reckless gamble, doomed to end in personal ruin?

Many explanations are possible. There is one explanation, however, that must not be overlooked. Says the famous Dr. Erich Lindemann of Harvard Medical School: "A good many forms of suicide or suicidal tendencies are the consequences of profound guilt feelings over deeds for which only death seems to be the appropriate restitution." [1]

The more we learn about human personality, the more we realize the havoc that can be wrought by a sense of guilt. Only those who are afflicted by it can understand the torment of the Psalmist when he cried in agony: [2]

> *"I know my transgressions,*
> *And my sin is ever before me."*

Not only psychiatrists but rabbis are familiar with the multitudes who suffer from this affliction. "And my sin is ever before me"—what a source of torture that can be!

Here is a fine woman whose life is periodically interrupted by fits of depression and moods of melancholy. Here is a man, on the surface successful, who whips himself, though unaware of it, for sins of commission or omission, real or imaginary. Here is a young son or daughter in bereavement, consumed by remorse for not having been more kind or tender or

1. Lindemann, Dr. Erich: Encyclopedia of Mental Health, *Guilt Feelings.*
2. Psalms 51:5.

attentive to a parent. And how many people do we know who are accident-prone; who are preoccupied with danger to their life and health; who are eaten up with hostility and who explode into violent aggressions of every variety.

Let these people speak what is in their hearts, and before long the secret is out. We are dealing with troubled souls, with personalities infested with rankling feelings of guilt. Wherever they turn it is the same: "And my sin is ever before me."

What can a rabbi contribute by way of relief for this malady? What technique, even mildly helpful, can he suggest?

The first suggestion to those who would cope with a sense of guilt is—exposure. Smoke it out! For as long as a sense of guilt remains concealed within the crevices of the soul, it fumes and festers and produces toxins that all but suffocate human personality. A guilt feeling is like a smouldering brand. It has to be dragged out into the open so that the drafts of reason may get at it and extinguish it.

If properly used, Yom Kippur can be the occasion for the employment of this technique. It is the one day of the year when man stands spiritually naked before his Maker. "Naught is hidden from Thee, nor is anything concealed from Thy sight." This is what we say on Yom Kippur as we share with God our most intimate secrets.

But if we are going to use this day to dispose once and for all of our guilt feelings, we had better do it right. Sometimes I wonder whether the neatly arranged prayers, the alphabetically organized confessions and the acrostically composed meditations really perform the purpose intended. I have the feeling that many worshippers miss the point entirely.

Here is what happens. We recount our sins as they are listed in the liturgy. We read them like a train schedule, and with as much enthusiasm. Then we remind ourselves, as it were, that this schedule is for week days only and does not include Saturdays and legal holidays. Besides, it is the wrong schedule: it expired on Labor Day.

The schedule of *al het* is simply not complete; certainly not sufficiently explicit. Small wonder then that our sages insist that on this day "man must specify the sin." He must particularize it, underscore it and emphasize it. Otherwise he will stand bowed, as the posture of confession requires, pound his breast rhythmically, as tradition prescribes, and all the while his guilt feelings will be showing.

That is not the way to deal with a sense of guilt. *"Hakoras ha'het"*—identification of the sin—is what Maimonides requires. This was not only the supreme Talmudist in him speaking but also the profound philosopher and the skilled physician. We must expose the things that we are afraid of, and we must reveal the things that we are ashamed to speak about.

Let a teacher of Judaism, on the holiest night of the year, dare to enumerate some of those things. How faithful have we been as husbands and wives? How understanding have we been as parents? How respectful have we been as children? How honest have we been in business? How indulgent have we been with ourselves and how frugal in our charity to others? How pious have we been in our hearts beyond the formal ritualism of our faith?

Let us read further from the catalogue of real sins—from another section of it. How touched are we by the plight of our people; by the catastrophe of Algerian Jewry; by the perils of those in benighted Arab lands? How concerned are we for the fate of the once proud and intellectually aristocratic Russian Jewry, now threatened by brutal extinction?

And here is another section: How intense is our Jewishness; how strong our loyalty to the traditions of our fathers; how genuine is our pride in the existence of a Jewish State? Do we honestly feel that three days a year in the Synagogue are sufficient to replenish our parched souls? And our children, what about them? Will a Sunday School education, or a trifle more, provide for their spiritual needs as Jews in the modern world?

And here is still another section: Are we aware of the alarming increase in inter-marriage; of the rising rate of outright apostasy; of the utter renunciation of their faith by droves of our young? What are we as parents doing about it? Are *we* setting the right example? Are our homes kosher; Jewishly warm; spiritually inspiring? Is there in them the glow of the Sabbath, the joy of festivals, the gaiety of holidays, the moral steadfastness of a father, the sweet and simple piety of a mother?

What has happened to our homes? Do they merely provide board and lodging for those who share the same address? Will they continue to be symbols of Jewish family solidarity— family solidarity without which Judaism cannot live and society cannot survive? Where, if not in the home, will children find anchorage and stability? Where, if not in the home, will they learn courtesy, decency, integrity, charity, kindness, hospitality and all the other noble ideals and attributes, without which the world is a jungle and human beings are virtual beasts of prey?

These are some of the things that we have to get off our chests. Everyone of us is bearing a heavy burden of guilt. Let us expose it to ourselves; let us reveal it to God. And as we do it, we will find relief. As the heart is unburdened, Isaiah promises us, healing will come.[3]

But exposure or identification of the guilt feeling is not enough. We must do more. We must be prepared to face the consequences. For real guilt there are real penalties. We refer

3. Isaiah 6:10.

to these penalties as "paying our debt to society." For a sense of guilt there are no penalties imposed from without. But there is a penalty prescribed from within. We call it penance. Penance is a means of paying a debt to oneself.

In the olden days, people who were obsessed by a sense of guilt would consult a rabbi; as a rule a Chassidic one. The Rabbi would prescribe a form of penance for them. The penance might have involved deprivation of certain pleasures, a regimen of prayers and psalms, submission to certain indignities, fasting or other forms of self-imposed mortification. A modern man might smile at such a system of penance. And perhaps it is a little naive for our day.

But here is an example of such penance in a modern form. Suppose a man were to sit down with his son or daughter and engage in a conversation like this: "My child, you are having difficulties. Doubts and fears assail you. You are subject to spasms of rage and to periods of melancholy. Your standards of value are wrong. Your moral patterns are lopsided. But, my child, the fault is not entirely yours. I am to blame in great measure. Perhaps I did not give you enough time. Maybe I did not display sufficient affection. Perhaps your insecurity is the result of my own instability. If you have failed me, then it is because I might have failed you."

What a dialogue that would be! By such humbleness a father would perform an act of penance! At the sight of such parental humility, a child might take fresh pride in his father and discover new love for him and, simultaneously, design a better pattern of life for himself.

Here is an example of such penance right out of Scripture:

The mighty King David had quite a career as a monarch in Israel. There were many things he did that simply wouldn't pass review. The establishment of his monarchy involved beating down enemies, destroying contenders, eliminating rivals. It is true that our sages never regarded David as a sinner.[4] Nonetheless, he was obsessed by a sense of guilt. "And my sin is ever before me," said he. He tried to atone for it, not merely by reciting, but by composing psalms and prayers. He even sought to still his conscience by proposing to build a Temple to God. He was rebuffed. "Your hands are stained with blood." In the Jewish tradition one cannot buy absolution.

Finally, in the language of the Talmud, God said to David, "How long will this sin lie concealed within you?"[5] Take your punishment and observe your penance. And David did. It was a severe penance that he chose, and a costly one. But in the end the sense of guilt that had troubled him throughout a lifetime was gone. His old age was serene, and at life's end ". . . David lay down with his ancestors," at peace with himself and at peace with eternity.

Smile not, therefore, at penance. It provides the best relief from the devastating disease of self-guilt. No external agency can be of help. Man himself must deal with self-guilt. His anguish is his penance. His aching heart, unburdened to the full, is his ultimate relief.

There is one further technique that may enable us to cope with a sense of guilt. It is a radical technique. It involves a total revision of our evaluation of man, of his nature, of his capacity and of his potentiality.

The prevailing philosophy of our day is guilt-centered. Unconsciously we have come to accept the Christian doctrine of Original Sin. The existentialist literature of our day, from Kierkegaard to Niebuhr, is completely preoccupied with sin. The sinfulness of man and his depravity have become the dominant themes in a whole symphony of gloom. Man, we are told, is born with the ineradicable stain of sin. His life is a

4. Sabbath 55b.
5. Sanhedrin 95a.

hopeless struggle against the power and torment of sin. His death is a welcome opportunity to be purged of sin.

This whole thought pattern is entirely un-Jewish. Jewish tradition, in the language of the popular song, "accentuates the positive and minimizes the negative." In our religion, the emphasis is not upon "*averah*"—sin, but upon "*mitzvah*"—the righteous act. We hold that man by disposition desires to be good. "The soul which Thou implanted in me is pure," says the Jew in his prayers every morning. Stamped with the image of God, man's highest striving is to imitate God. Man's feet may drag him towards the swamps of wickedness, but his soul lifts him towards the heavens. To be sure, there are "evil drives" that push him downward, but there are even stronger "good drives" that propel him upward. A Chassidic Rabbi observed that man may be compared to a rope, one end of which is pulled by God and the other by Satan. It is obvious who must be the victor in this tug-of-war.

If that be so, then just as the sense of guilt is the residue of the guilt act, so can the sense of righteousness be the product of the righteous act. The guilt complex is in a sense the ashes that remain after the fires of sin have burned down. The "mitzvah-complex" may be compared to the embers that glow after the flames of righteousness have set a personality ablaze.

What a consoling thought this is for the individual. Man is told that he can be good. In fact, he is told that it is easier to be good than to be bad. To be a good husband is easier than to be a bad one. To be a loving wife is more pleasant than to be a nagging one. To lavish affection upon children is more rewarding than to withhold it. To be kind requires less exertion than to be cruel. To be charitable takes less effort than to be niggardly. To love one's people is more natural than to deny them. To acknowledge one's identity with his faith and culture is far more honorable than to abandon them. In a word, it is easier for a human being to be a man than to be a savage.

If man takes this easier path towards goodness, he will not be troubled by a sense of guilt. His reward will be a sense of righteousness.

11 &

Coping With the Problem
of Fear

Some two decades ago, when Nazi tyranny threatened the entire world, a great American President lifted the drooping spirits of his people with the words: "We have nothing to fear but fear."

Before him a wise French thinker phrased it almost similarly: "The thing in the world," said Montaigne, "that I am most afraid of, is fear . . ."

Long before anyone recognized the universality of this emotion, the Bible spoke of it after its own fashion. Says the Psalmist: "There they were in great fear, where no fear there was . . ." [1]

When we deal with the problem of fear, therefore, we are dealing with the most obsessive emotion of the human personality. Psychiatrists have identified at least fifteen varieties of fear that may afflict a human being. There is no one who at one time or another in his life was not afraid. We are afraid of the dark; we are afraid of growing old; we are afraid of becoming poor; we are afraid of illness; we are afraid of death. In a word, as the Bible puts it: "And you shall be afraid by night and by day . . ."

1. Psalms 53:6.

In our day fear has become the professional domain of psychiatry. From the day that Sigmund Freud treated what came to be known as the case of "little Hans," psychologists and analysts tried to understand the reasons that lay behind fears and anxieties, and their efforts brought relief and healing to many a tormented soul. Let these intrepid explorers of the human mind continue their earnest efforts and persistent researches.

Religion, however, is equally concerned with the problem of fear. There are some who would even cynically suggest that fear is what brought religion into being. Primitive man, they argue, was afraid of the dark, of the forest, of hunger, of his enemies. And so he created God as a sort of cosmic handyman to help him and to protect him. By now, this fanciful interpretation of religion is thoroughly rejected as so much claptrap.

But cynicism aside, true religion has always been concerned with the fears and anxieties of human beings. Man always turned to religion to refresh a wilting personality and to seek fortification against the natural terrors of life. "Heal me, O Lord, for I am frightened." [2] This was and remains the universal cry of the anguished heart of man, and it is directed to the heart of religion.

Is it not of some significance that this holiday season is traditionally referred to as the *Yamim Noraim?* The usual translation is "the days of awe." Perhaps these are also the days when we ought to deal with people who are *awed*, with men and women who are scared, with a whole world that dwells in terror.

Terror is, indeed, the mood of mankind today. From the Congo to Cuba and from Berlin to Buenos Aires, men are agitated by fear. It is not revolution that is in the air, but panic. We are not in pursuit of anything, but in flight from every-

2. Psalms 6:3.

thing. Even the astronauts orbiting our globe are propelled by the fear and nervousness of the nations that send them aloft. We are reaching for the moon, because we cannot stand the quakes and tremors of our earth.

In an atmosphere of global terror, what chance has the individual for mental peace and serenity? The news that he reads across his breakfast table can destroy his digestion for the whole day. Atomic explosions above ground and under ground, above water and under water, cause him to shake and shiver. In a state of prolonged cold war, the emotional temperature of men cannot remain normal. Otherwise, how can one explain the behavior of our fellow citizens in Mississippi? There, fear has brought on the inevitable emotional consequence—rage and hate. The word "phobia" has a double meaning: fear and hate. All of the racial tensions the world over are not merely the result of social, economic and political factors. Fundamentally, they are the emotional reactions of scared and terrified people, whose outlet is rage, hate and violence. "Heal me, O Lord, for I am frightened."

What healing then can religion provide for the scared souls of men? How can it quiet their fears and allay their anxieties?

For one thing, religion can correct our perspective of fear. We are naturally inclined to look upon any crisis or danger in our lives at close range. The crisis then looms large and foreboding; the danger appears imminent and immediate. The result is fright, shock and panic, followed by emotional turmoil and mental wretchedness.

It is remarkable that Scripture long ago recognized this reaction to fear. The Bible speaks of "a trembling heart and failing eyes." [3] When the heart trembles, the vision becomes blurred. If only we could see our fears in proper focus! If only we could take a time exposure of our phobias!

When we consider the perils of life from the vantage point

3. Deut. 28:65.

of long-range human experience, they take on an altogether different complexion. Not all fear is abnormal. Some fears are healthy, constructive and creative. Let us list some of them.

For ages men were afraid of the dark. That fear quickened the discovery of fire and light. Fear of illness and pain made possible the miracle of medicine. Fear of hunger produced agriculture. Fear of loneliness created society. Fear of devils and demons resulted in the quest for God. Fear of solitude begot love. Fear of tyrants gave birth to democracy and brought liberty into the world.

In the light of historical perspective, some fears turned out to be blessings. The fears to which mankind is exposed today may bring similar results. Even the ominous satellites whirling in space today may become the Telestars of tomorrow, projecting song, heralding peace and filling the cosmos with hymns of glory and melodies of brotherhood. The Prophet Isaiah may have had that in mind when he said: "And your heart will tremble and will expand." [4] In other words, fear need not depress or constrict. It may release the adrenal juices of the personality and induce expansiveness, excitement and hope.

Our analysis of the character of fear leads to a further conclusion. Fear is inertia. It is a paralysis of the will, an excuse for passivity, a defense against action, a surrender to indifference, a resistance to effort.

There is a beautiful legend associated with the dream ladder of Jacob. [5] Jacob saw the princes of many nations mounting the ladder of his dreams as he lay asleep. God stood over him and urged him on, "Awake and climb." But Jacob hesitated. "I am afraid," said he, "lest I fall even as others do." And even God's insistence could not move him. The legend ends with a divine rebuke for his cowardice.

What a precious lesson this sad but lovely legend contains.

4. Isaiah 60:5.
5. Lev. R. Ch. 29.

Psychiatry has a Greek name for the fear of high places. It is called acrophobia. But what matters is not the name, but the tragedy—the fear to climb, the horror of attaining heights, the terror of falling.

And so, many lie dreaming sweet dreams of lofty ladders that others are mounting. They see beautiful visions of beckoning heights. They hear imploring urgings to rise. "Awake and climb," says the small still voice. But to no avail. "I am afraid lest I fall . . ." is the feeble response.

Promising careers remain unfulfilled; lofty ambitions are never realized; great loves are never enjoyed; happy marriages are never consummated; the laughter of children is never heard; the thrill of adventure is never savored; the drama of life is concluded ere the final act is reached. A frightened sleeper is one morning found alone—an empty vial of pills at his side. "Heal me, O Lord, for I am frightened."

There is another version to the Jacob legend here recounted. That version has a happy ending and that happy ending is made possible by religion.[6] Jacob did arise in response to the divine call. He was assured that even as God's glory is infinite, so are man's potentialities endless. Man's courage to realize his potentialities must never falter or fail. His ascent has no limits, for the ladder of life reaches towards heaven.

A good friend and a successful analyst concludes his learned article on phobias with two possible epitaphs for a patient ridden with fears.[7] Here is the first:

She couldn't try
For fear she'd die;
She never tried
And so she died.

And here is the second:

6. Ex. R. Ch. 32:4.
7. Friedman, Paul: *American Handbook of Psychiatry*, Ch. 15, p. 304.

She couldn't try
For fear she'd die;
But once she tried
Her fears—they died.

These lines are psychiatric in content, but religious in spirit. "Over every blade of grass stands an angel and commands— 'grow, sprout'." Over every person stands someone—a parent, teacher, friend, his *alter ego*, his true and better self, and urges—arise and fear not; reach out and attain; advance and arrive.

How far have we come in the analysis of our thought? We have seen that religion puts fear into its proper perspective, so that man may see it as a common, continuous and universal experience. We have also realized that religion demonstrates that great fears often produce great things. We have also concluded that religion is a goad and a challenge to man in his endless battle with fear.

But religion can do even more. It can perform a more direct and salutary role in coping with the problem of fear.

Religion builds character. It thus provides the inner resources of personality with those attributes that are essential to meet the challenges of life. It thus enables man to roll with the punches that life strikes and to absorb the inevitable traumas of existence. The magic word is—faith.

Of course, faith is much misunderstood. People think of it as resignation, passivity and surrender. Nothing is further from the truth, certainly from the truth of Judaism. Man is not a helpless tool in the hands of an inexorable destiny.

Nor is faith blind credulity. People generally set up reason against faith as though the two were opposed to each other. Faith is not unreasonable, nor can reason stand without faith. Let us put it this way—faith is the logic of the soul, and logic is the faith of the mind.

Such faith is man's choicest asset. Within its orbit fear simply melts away. Through its power—and faith is power— doubt is transformed into confidence. Under its spell despair is turned into hope.

Without faith man could never have accepted the challenge of the forces of nature or fathomed the mystery of life. He would not have dared to grapple with darkness and to invent light. He would have remained scared of the unknown and would not have conceived God. He would have curbed his curiosity and would have left unexplored the remote frontiers of existence.

William James reports that as a medical student he was terrified by the dissection room and was in morbid fear of his courses in anatomy. Were it not for the twenty-third Psalm, he would have given up or gone mad. That didn't happen, because he heard the accents of faith: "Though I walk in the valley of the shadow of death, I shall fear no evil; for Thou art with me."

Moses was "afraid to look at God," but he heard the summons of faith: "Come up to Me, on the mountain." It was then that the Lawgiver was born and the Commandments came into the possession of mankind.

Millions of our people were exposed to terrors and horrors never before known. Yet at the entrance to gas chambers and on the very threshold of death the echoes of a millenial faith reverberated through all the jungles of Nazidom as fearless men chanted: "I believe in the coming of the Messiah." It is this courage, nurtured by faith, that enabled a people to survive, a nation to be reborn and a state to be re-established.

"The Lord is my light and my salvation; whom shall I fear? The Lord is the fortress of my life; of whom shall I be afraid?" [8] This is faith; but this is therapy as well.

"He maketh me lie down in green pastures; he leadeth me beside the still waters." [9] What therapist can do more for a patient suffering from agoraphobia, the fear of open spaces.

8. Psalms 27:1.
9. Psalms 23:2.

Even Freud approves this technique in order to build up the
patient's confidence.

"Fear not, for I am with thee; be not dismayed for I am
your God; I will strengthen thee and help thee . . ." [10]
Those words are part of the vocabulary of faith. If one is
fluent in such vocabulary; if the lexicon of religion is his daily
handbook, he will need little else.

10. Isaiah 41:10.

12 ❧

The Flight from One's Self

The flight from one's self is a common phenomenon of our restless age. In an unsteady world, man can hardly be expected to remain intact and integrated. When life is in nervous movement, man is inevitably "on the run." And it is such a condition that the Bible described when it said, "And ye shall run, with no one pursuing you." [1]

In its pathological forms this flight from one's self is one of the maladies of personality. But our concern is not with these forms. Our psychology-conscious generation is familiar with persecution complexes, amnesias, hallucinations and other varieties of flights from reality. Their causes lie deep within the caverns of the subconscious. Their diagnosis is the province of the skilled psychiatrist. Their cure is, alas, not always certain. Our hearts must feel sympathy for those who are afflicted with that ancient curse, "And ye shall run, with no one pursuing you."

The concern of a teacher of religion is with the more common and, fortunately, the less malignant forms of flights from one's self. For a flight from reality need not necessarily be a long-distance, non-stop excursion. It can be made in a series of short hops. But at every point along the route the "I" and the

1. Lev. 26:17.

97

"me" draw further apart until they are no longer the personal pronouns of the same person.

As one contemplates this problem, he is struck at once by its universality. In one form or another, to one degree or another, at some time or another, everyone of us seeks escape from himself. A drink to forget; a new hat to change the lady's mood; a journey to get away from it all—are some of the innocent manifestations of the desire to flee from reality. All are subject to it—the beautiful and the uncomely, the wealthy and the poor, the affluent and the humble. One may resort to the metaphor of the day and observe that the flight from one's self is not exclusively a coach flight; luxury accommodations can also be had. Indeed, all of us run with no one pursuing us.

If this experience is universal, then why is it so? What are the causes that make so many resort to flight from themselves?

The first cause is a sense of guilt. "The wicked flee when no man pursueth," [2] says the author of the book of Proverbs. Even our modern courts are impressed by that. Flight in itself is often regarded as an acknowledgment of guilt. In the affairs of life there are so many "hit and run" drivers. A moral error is committed. False pride prevents confession. The ego will not permit exposure. Yet the soul of man is plagued and tortured, and the resultant anguish manifests itself in fears and anxieties that make life intolerable. Some form of escape— cowardly and futile, to be sure—becomes inevitable.

Another cause for flight from one's self is dissatisfaction with one's self. There are many who do not like themselves. And since they know themselves better than anyone else does, they might be right at that. They would prefer to be as pretty or as healthy or as wise as someone they know. That is why Americans spent half a billion dollars on cosmetics last year.

2. Proverbs 28:1.

That is why we torture ourselves with all sorts of diets. That is why we seek a quick road to knowledge and are anxious to acquire wisdom in five easy lessons. Since such methods hardly achieve the desired purpose, man indulges in self-pity or in rebellion against himself, or in hatred of himself—or escape from himself.

Oftentimes this dissatisfaction with one's self finds a rather strange outlet. The outlet is imitation. Since we do not like ourselves, we try to be like someone else. We will follow someone else's taste in clothes; we will imitate someone else's social manners; we will even mimic someone else's accent. We think that by these methods we achieve a new personality, more attractive, more impressive, more desirable than our own.

How absurd and ridiculous our conduct becomes is obvious only to those about us. And as with other malodorous conditions, even our best friends won't tell us. For imitation is in normal conduct what hallucination is in abnormal behavior. While it may be a form of flattery to the one imitated, it is an acknowledgment of self-hatred on the part of the imitator. It is possible that Emerson meant just that when he said that "imitation is suicide." For is it not, in fact, a destruction of one's true self?

Certainly, as Jews, we ought to be familiar with this. Self-hatred is, alas, not uncommon among us, and imitation of others is not an infrequent expression of it. For eighteen centuries we suffered because we were Jews. Shame was our portion and humiliation our lot. The weak among us could not for long endure it. They resorted to concealing their identity and denying their ancestry. They performed plastics on their faces, which may have been excusable. But they attempted plastics on their personalities by imitating those about them. "Let us be like all nations, O Israel," [3] they said. "Be a Jew at

3. Ezekiel 20:32.

home and a man away from home" became their slogan. Imitation or, as it was more commonly known, assimilation was elevated to a philosophy of life. What a shameful philosophy! For whom did they imitate but their traducers, persecutors and humiliators?

Some consciously, or unconsciously, persist in this undignified policy of imitation. They abandon an ancient cultural heritage and maintain but tenuous ties with our faith. They deprive their children of a Jewish education and launch them upon a career of imitation by sending them off to what they think is a fashionable private school, whose distinction lies in its tolerance of a few Jewish students to whom it grants grudging admission. They limit their contact with our religion to a few days a year. They condescendingly partake of an occasional "kosher style" meal and then heap scorn on what they regard as "gastronomic Judaism." When the State of Israel is in the headlines, they are thrown into a panic of fear lest their patriotism be suspect. "Let us be like all the nations, O Israel" is still their credo of cowardice and fear.

And whom are we imitating? Whom did the assimilationist German Jew imitate for a century? Whom would the American Council for Judaism imitate—Governor Faubus and the hoodlums of Little Rock? The White Christians of the South who are as black in their morality as they are un-Christian in their religion?

No, imitation, whether individual or collective, is a symptom of self hate and a most undignified attempt to escape from one's self. In the final analysis we can never imitate one whom we cannot truly resemble. By persisting in our imitation we become counterfeits and no more.

There is yet another cause to explain the flight from one's self. It is lack of confidence in one's self. "Who am I that I should go to Pharaoh?," asked a hesitant Moses. Pharaoh will not receive me; the children of Israel will not believe me; and, besides, I am so ill-equipped for the mission ". . . for I am slow of speech and heavy of tongue." If this lack of confidence had been permitted to go unchallenged, what a calamity for mankind. No Moses, no Ten Commandments, no "proclaim liberty throughout the land to all the inhabitants thereof!" Indeed, no western civilization as we know it!

Or listen to a terrified Isaiah as he is summoned to his calling. "Woe is me! for I am undone because I am a man of unclean lips . . ." [4] Had his lack of confidence been final, where would humanity have heard

> *"And they shall beat their swords into plowshares,*
> *And their spears into pruning hooks;*
> *Nation shall not lift up sword against nation,*
> *Neither shall they learn war any more."*

One impressive fact must now be apparent. It is simply impossible to run away from one's self. Such flight is futile. The "I" and the "me" are wedded for life. No divorce is possible. The strands that, woven together, form the pattern of personality are inextricably intertwined. Unravel them and the pattern is damaged and the personality becomes blurred or faded or destroyed. Paraphrasing the Psalmist, man had better say to himself, "Whither shall *I* go from *me* or where shall I flee from *my* presence?" There is no flight from one's self, no escape from conscience, no desertion of destiny.

Our sacred literature abounds in examples of those who thought that they could make good their escape from themselves. Our patriarch Jacob, as a young man, thought so. "And Jacob fled into the fields of Aram," [5] is the way the Bible metaphorically puts it. By nature, Jacob was "a humble man dwelling in tents." Our sages described him as a man of piety and as a dedicated student. Then, in the exuberance of

4. Isaiah 6:5.
5. Hosea 12:1.

youth, he probably thought that such a life was not for him. So off he ran into the wide opportunities of Mesopotamia. There he could become a rich herdsman. There his cunning uncle Laban would teach him all the tricks of business. He could even buy the love of Rachel and Leah. One day he would corner the entire cattle market. His plans for success were fully realized. "For with my staff did I cross this Jordan, and now I am become two companies." [6] Not one corporation, mind you, but two! The new Jacob was a resounding success.

But the new Jacob just could not run away from the old Jacob. The split personality had to be mended. Here is the true Jacob speaking after twenty years of flight from himself: "And the angel of God said to me in my dream, 'Jacob, Jacob . . . return to the land of thy birth.' " [7] Counting sheep will not bring you restful sleep. Return to your *self*.

Of course, the most classic example of attempted escape from one's self is the prophet Jonah. Apparently our tradition considered his experience so important that it included the story of his life in the prophetic portion read on Atonement Day. "And Jonah fled to Tarshish from God," Scripture tells us. By profession a prophet, he was assigned to perform a mission. But he fled from that which was his calling, his destiny and his true self. He did all the things that fugitives from themselves before him and after him had done in order to make good their escape. He concealed his identity and got himself, as it were, a false passport. He bought passage on a ship. According to one interpretation of our commentators, he paid for the entire ship.[8] The whole vessel became his deluxe cabin. Satisfied that he was safe and secure, he lay down and slept.

But, did he really sleep? The storms of conscience and the

6. Gen. 32:11.
7. Gen. 31:3.
8. Ned. 38a.

tempests of inner compulsion have a way of tossing one back to reality. There comes a moment when gnawing questions must be answered: ". . . what is your occupation; whence comest thou; what is thy country; and of what people art thou?" [9] In a word, who are you and are you faithful to your true self?

What was the end of the episode? "And the Lord spoke to Jonah a second time. Arise and go into Nineveh . . . and proclaim there what I bid thee." Once again a split personality was mended—a fugitive prophet came back to himself.

The Zohar, repository of mystic lore, saw a parallel between Jonah as a type and man as a creature of life. "Jonah descending into the ship is symbolic of man's soul, that descends into this world to enter his body." [10] The soul is the *self* of man. It cannot be silenced or squelched. It permits neither flight nor fancy. It tolerates neither escape nor evasion. When one seeks to flee from it, it harpoons him, alas, sometimes at great pain, back into the shielding net of his personality.

A concluding word must here be spoken. Yom Kippur is that magic day when man can make the return back to himself. The process by which that is done is theologically called repentance. It is strange that the word "repent" comes from a Greek root, which means to crawl or creep back. In the Hebrew the word has greater dignity. It is "Teshuva," and it means *return*.

On Yom Kippur a Jew stands before his God, without powder or paint, without mask or disguise. He stands not as an imitator, nor as a mimic. He divests himself of all the trappings of superficiality, of all sham and make-believe. He stands before his Maker with his true self bare and exposed.

On Atonement Day men and women look about and see

9. Jonah 1:8.
10. Zohar, Exodus 198.

their children and wonder whether they might have escaped the responsibilities and obligations of true fatherhood and motherhood. They look upon each other, and they wonder if they might not have fled from the embrace of glorious love, from the idyllic beauty of husbandhood and wifehood, to wallow in the marshes of looseness and infidelity.

On Atonement Day man looks up to his God, who gave him his soul, pure and inviolate, and which he, by his misdeeds, may have polluted. He draws closer to his ancient people, identity with which he might have sought to deny. Never are man or woman, Jew or Jewess, as much themselves as they are on this Holy Day.

What, then, in our spiritual nakedness, shall we say to ourselves at this hour? It must be this: The flight from myself is ended. I have flown high and far and fast. Apparently it was not fast enough to escape, not far enough to find release, not high enough to reach the unreachable. My flaps are lowered in humility; my landing gear is set. Weary and worn from my odyssey, I beg you, O Lord, to guide me from your observation tower. I am coming in on a wing and a prayer. "O God, bring me back and let me return . . ."

13

The Art of Self-Discovery

Of all discoveries the most momentous is self-discovery. The ancient explorers knew the thrill that came after weary months of wandering when on the distant horizon they sighted the goal of their journey and could hilariously cry out, "Land, ahoy!"

Greater still is the joy that comes to a man who, after being tossed about aimlessly on the sea of existence, peers one day into the very heart of his being, through the fog and mist that envelop it, and is able to exclaim, "Man, ahoy!" He has found himself.

Yet men are reluctant to embark upon a voyage of self-discovery. They will launch expeditions to the furthermost reaches of the earth and venture into the staggering distances of the space all about it. Before long the moon and other planets will yield their secrets to the intrepid curiosity of man. Yes, man will explore everything and everywhere except that which is nearest to him—himself, his heart, his soul.

The Psalmist once pleaded for such self-discovery. "Search me, O God," he prayed, "and know my heart; examine me and know my thoughts." [1] This is what all of us should ask

1. Psalms 139:23.

for. With the popular poet, a preacher would like to say on this holy night:

"Confront yourself and look you in the eye—
Just stand aside and watch yourself go by."

In other words, let us stop collecting the portraits of others, and let us sit down for our own portrait—a self-portrait.

To educate men in the art of self-discovery is one of the great responsibilities of religion. It was always so. For long before psychoanalysis, religion already taught self-analysis. In the truest sense, that is what confession was meant to be. I do not mean the kind of confession whereby one divulges his misdeeds and transgressions to a specially ordained functionary. Judaism never required an intermediary, or a religious runner, between man and God, who reports, as it were, that someone was unloading a heavy load of sin at the best possible heavenly quotation on absolutions.

There is another kind of confession. Man confronts himself as if he were looking into a mirror and says, in the language of our prayer, "What am I? What is my life . . . What is my righteousness . . . What is my strength . . . What is my salvation . . . ?" He asks these questions rhetorically of God, but actually of himself. Through them he hopes to solve the riddle of his existence. For as he posits these questions, he is in the deepest sense questing after the purpose of life. He is engaged in an exercise of self-examination that may lead to self-discovery. "Search me, O God, and know my heart; examine me and know my thoughts."

Let us immediately set down a rather apparent but necessary truth. Until self-discovery takes place, life has no direction. A person has got to know whither he wants to go if he ever expects to get there. It is so simple a fact, yet so frequently overlooked.

Recall the biblical episode of Hagar fleeing from her mistress Sarah. An angel meets her and asks her, "Hagar . . . whence comest thou and whither goest thou?" And Hagar answers, "From Sarah my mistress am I fleeing." [2] Is it not strange—two questions were asked, "Whence comest thou and whither goest thou." But only one answer was given, "From Sarah my mistress am I fleeing." For the second question Hagar had no answer. Lacking purpose, she also lacked direction.

How many of us are in that category. Not knowing where to go, we get nowhere fast. Having no goal in mind, we reach no objective in space. When an inner voice asks us—whither goest thou, we can only answer that we are fleeing from some place. Let us be honest with ourselves. Is it wealth that we are seeking, or poverty that we are running from? Is it pleasure that we are craving, or loneliness that we are escaping? Is it prominence that we strive for, or inferiority that we are evading? Is it love that we yearn for, or rejection that we fear? Is it marriage we want, or insecurity that we dread? Is it a mate that we desire, or a parent that we would renounce? God, why can we not see that without self-discovery life has no direction. Life becomes a oneway street with a dead end.

A second truth suggests itself. Until self-discovery takes place, man is incapable of full and true realization. The religious literature of the Jew is full with proof of that.

Remember the story of Jacob as he left the home of his father-in-law, Laban. After twenty years of labor he had become a man of great fortune and the head of a large household. The Bible has him saying at that point, ". . . For with my staff did I cross this Jordan and behold I have become two companies." A poor fugitive lad who left his father's home penniless became in a relatively short time an Eastern po-

2. Gen. 16:8.

tentate, a Messopotamian tycoon, the proud proprietor of two corporations. Not bad, Jacob, not bad at all!

Yet it was precisely at the moment when he took inventory of his material success that a peculiar fear gripped him. "And Jacob feared greatly and became distressed . . ." [3] Why at that moment? Had he not found the clue to wealth? Had he not learned the formula of success? He even discovered a biologic trick whereby white sheep could give birth to spotted sheep. Yes, he discovered all that. But somehow he never, till that moment, stopped to look into his own soul and to discover himself.

The Bible describes this personality crisis most dramatically. "And Jacob was left alone, and a man wrestled with him till the break of day." [4] What a wrestling match this was! What a wrestling match it always is when man grapples with his own soul, seeking to discover his true self. Jacob found himself. He discovered the true purpose of life. He shed the name Jacob and took on the title Israel, which henceforth would define his mission and destiny—one who contends against men and gods, and prevails.

What a discovery it is when man discovers himself, and what consequences result from it!

Let us think of yet another illustration to emphasize this truth. Even Moses had to go through this process of self-discovery before he could become the supreme emancipator and the divine law-giver of all time. Happily married to the beautiful daughter of Jethro, he could have remained the keeper of his father-in-law's flocks and a proud member of one of the best families of Midyan. Then one day he was attracted by the sight of a burning bush. "Let me draw near and behold this strange sight; wherefore does not the bush burn?" [5] A thorn bush is enveloped in flame and is not con-

3. Gen. 32:8.
4. Gen. 32:25.
5. Exodus 3:31.

sumed! How it made him think! Perhaps there is something indestructible, even though it be inflammable, in man. What is it? How can one get at that inflammable something that can burn, light, heat, and yet not consume? How can one kindle such a flame in others—yes, even in a whole world?

Out of this deep reflection came self-discovery. A voice called, "Moses, Moses," and an answer came, "Here I am." A man discovered himself. What a man he became, and what great things he wrought!

Examine further the pages of history, and you will continue to find countless examples of this truth. At forty an ignorant Palestinian discovered himself and, as a result of such self-discovery, became the renowned Rabbi Akiba, greatest of Talmudic sages, noblest of ethical teachers and most heroic martyr of our people.

A humble rail splitter looked into his soul by the dim light of a fireplace in a modest log cabin, and what he saw made him become the great emancipator, Abraham Lincoln.

An aristocrat of Judea searched his heart and then left the grandeur of his surroundings to become the prophet of universal peace and brotherhood, Isaiah.

A young Schubert, of whom a biographer says that "his creative fever burned him up in his thirty-first year," reached an understanding of life's meaning, and out of poverty and tragedy he distilled the "Unfinished Symphony," symbol by its very name of the endless possibilities of human genius when it discovers itself.

A man in the prime of life discovers his true self while in the dark throes of a crippling polio, and converts a wheel chair into a throne, a crutch into a mighty sword and, although unable to walk himself, leads an entire world to glorious victory.

O, what greatness results when man discovers himself!

"Search me, Oh God, and know my heart. Examine me and know my thoughts."

By now it must be evident that the first and most indispensable technique in the art of self-discovery is introspection. No man ever discovered himself without probing deeply into his own personality. First he must lay his soul bare to his own scrutiny. He has to assess his powers and evaluate his deficiencies. He must examine his achievements and consider his failures. He must draw an honest balance sheet of his accomplishments and fearlessly set down all his liabilities.

Having done that, he must decide what he wants out of life. There are several extremely penetrating questions that he must ask of himself. What do I honestly think of myself? Never mind what others think of me. Am I concerned with self-worth, or am I, as alas many of us are, a dizzy social climber? What do I cherish more, a good book and a good friend or the glamour and tinsel of a superficial life? These are very painful questions. They dig right into the flesh and substance of personality. They are not easy to ask and even more difficult to answer. They require courage and honesty.

Yet it is upon the answers to these questions that self-discovery depends. It was the famous philosopher, George Santayana, who said, "nothing requires a rarer intellectual heroism than the willingness to see one's own equation written out." If that is a little too philosophical for some of us, let us put it in simpler terms. *What* plus *what* equals you? *What* minus *what* is responsible for a poorer you? *What* multiplied by *what* will produce a better you?

Such introspection will lead to self-discovery. Yet not all of us are capable of it. For those who are not, it becomes the duty of a teacher of religion to suggest a somewhat simpler technique.

Here it is. If we cannot look scrutinizingly, fearlessly, into ourselves, then let us study carefully and painstakingly some-one else. The poet put it simply, thus:

"Just stand aside and watch yourself go by;
Think of yourself as he instead of I."

All about us are people. Let us observe them. Here is a man you admire. He is a prosperous businessman. He has achieved prominence in politics. He has won recognition socially. Of course, you would like to be like him. Now look carefully. Does he appear serene? Is he relaxed? Is his wife ever at his side? Are his children proud of him? Now decide. Would you like to be like him? And if you resemble him, would you want to continue to do so?

Or, here is a lady. She is beautiful in form and charming in manner. She is well-dressed and well-received. She is seen in the finest places and travels in the loveliest circles. Wouldn't you want to be like her? Now look carefully again. Is she "the woman of valor," whom the Book of Proverbs describes, "whose worth is more than that of rubies?" Do "her children rise up and call her blessed, her husband also, and he praiseth her saying, 'many daughters have done worthily, but thou excellest them all.' " Now, do you want to be like her? And if you are like her, would you want to continue? Upon the answer to these questions will depend your self-discovery.

All about us are such people from whom we can learn. Not all of us are skilled to probe our personalities with an instrument. Only the most heroic are capable of using a scalpel upon their souls. Everyone, however, can use a mirror. Other personalities perform the role of mirrors for us. It is in them that we see our own smudges or our own comeliness. It is through them, therefore, that we discover ourselves. How did Solomon put it? "As the water showeth to the face the reflected face, so doth the heart of man show itself to another man." [6]

There is yet a third technique whereby self-discovery may be achieved. It is through the identification of oneself with the fate and destiny of others. Let us put it epigrammatically. In order to find oneself, one must be capable of losing oneself. The best way of doing that is by absorption and identification with the total self of society. This, indeed, is the paradox of the matter. Only when one is truly selfless does he discover his true self.

This technique, too, is confirmed by history and ratified by experience. "And it came to pass that when Moses matured, he went forth to his brethren." When an Egyptian overseer lashed a Jew, Moses felt the pain. When a nation was driven into exile, a Jeremiah, who might have saved himself, trudged along with them, lamenting their sad fate. When a little child wept, Rabbi Israel Salanter could not pray. When a Negro was enslaved, Lincoln felt himself in chains. When a flower is exposed to the sun it achieves growth, beauty and fragrance. So is it with man. When he identifies himself with his fellow man he achieves purpose and fulfillment. Always when we lose ourselves in the needs of others, we find our true selves.

As Jews, we must especially learn this lesson. Some of us labor under a tragic illusion that the further we get away from our fellow Jews, the more we will be recognized for what we are. The argument runs something like this. Soft-pedal your Jewish identity; let the flimsiest bonds tie you to your ancestral faith; speak in subdued tones of the State of Israel; in other words, submerge yourself as a Jew in order that you may the better emerge as a man. O, how false such logic is! How can one emerge as a man when he has lost his manliness in the process of submerging his Jewishness.

6. Prov. 27:19.

When the famous Albert Einstein was acclaimed for his theory of relativity, Germany said he was a German and France said he belonged to the world. The great scientist reacted characteristically. Said he, "If my theory of relativity is proved correct, Germany will continue to claim me as a German and France will continue to say that I belong to the world. Should the theory, however, prove incorrect, France will say I am a German, and Germany will say I am a Jew."

What matters it what others think of you is the lesson of this story. Assert your Jewishness and you will be respected. Deny it and you have even lost the title to your manhood.

There is one final technique in the art of self-discovery. Man discovers himself when he realizes that there is someone above him. Without God, self-discovery is impossible.

It is a common error of secularist thinking that religion shackles a person, inhibits his will, represses his freedom and dulls his senses. Therefore, the secularist contends that the religious man is never himself. Well then, let us break the inhibitions, release the repressions, give free rein to the will, yield to the appetites. And what is the result? The result, my friends, is unconditional surrender to the lowest in man.

On the other hand, submission to God's will and purpose is not at all an act of surrender. It is rather the method by which one discovers the best, the finest and the noblest in man. When we pray to a God of mercy, compassion, love, do we not automatically assert that we consider these divine attributes as virtues deserving of imitation by us? God then becomes the cosmic mirror into which man looks in order that he may see himself better. He then begins to resemble God and to assume the divine image. And the more man becomes like God, the closer does he become the true man that he should be. When man finds God, he discovers himself.

Let us conclude the matter thus. There are three directions that one must follow on the exploratory expedition that leads to self-discovery. These directions are—inward, into oneself; outward, into society; upward, toward God.

14

The Art of Memory

There is good reason for the holiday of Rosh Hashanah to be called *Yom Hazikoron*—the Day of Remembrance. For as a new year is ushered in, it is so important to recall and to reflect upon the year and the years gone by. Only fools tear the pages off the calendar of life and cast them into the waste basket of oblivion. Wise men treasure those pages as precious memories which, like the fallen leaves of a tree, enrich the soil of life for future growth.

"I remember the days of old," [1] said King David, and indeed he did. He remembered and set down for all posterity the victories and the defeats, the moral lapses and the spiritual triumphs, the moments of depression and the periods of exaltation, the occasional doubts and the ultimate faith. He remembered the treachery of a son and the forgiveness of a father, the joys of a husband and the sorrows of a king, the fury of enemies and the devotion of friends. He remembered, and the repository of those memories is our greatest spiritual treasure, the Psalms of David.

Such memory is an art, and to the cultivation of that art a rabbi summons you on this Rosh Hashanah morning.

To be sure, the art of memory is one art that our genera-

1. Psalms 143:5.

tion would rather not cultivate. There is so much that our generation would rather forget. The wars, the tyrannies, the brutal extermination of millions, the futile appeasement of international hoodlums—we would like to forget all of that. The fact that half the world is starving while the other half is dieting—we would like to forget that too. The billions spent on armament and by proportion the pennies spent on cancer research—we would prefer to forget that too. In a word, the twentieth century would like to forget, because it is ashamed or afraid to remember. In the language of Job, "When I remember I am affrighted and horror takes hold on my flesh." [2]

That, of course, is consistent with the teachings of psychiatry. We forget what we do not choose to remember. What we overlook, however, is that, whether it be the individual or society, our relief lies in confronting our terror and shame, in understanding their cause, and in avoiding their recurrence. For our own peace of mind, we had better "remember the days of old."

A word of caution must be spoken at this point. There are memories that are best eradicated. There are experiences that clutter up the mind and leave scars upon the personality. There are, for example, grievances and hurts that some never forget, and their lives are spent brooding over them. There are errors and blunders that people commit and, instead of wiping them off clean from the slate of their memory, allow them to smolder and fester as ugly guilt feelings that poison their personalities.

Then there are the sick souls who just won't let go of their memories. They do not live *with* the past, but *in* the past. Life for them becomes a sort of cemetery, and they stand as perpetual mourners bowing over the tombstones of long interred yesteryears. In a remarkable passage the Talmud informs us that if a man continually reads the inscriptions upon tomb-

2. Job 21:6.

stones, his memory becomes dull.[3] How true that is! When David said, "I remember the days of old," he was recalling a life, not a graveyard.

It is time now to recognize certain positive realities about memory.

For one thing, without memory progress is impossible. For what in truth is memory if not the projection of an experience upon the screen of the mind, or the inscription of an event upon the tablet of the heart? If there were no memories, age after age would have to start from the beginning. In the odyssey of mankind from primitiveness to civilization, footprints were made in the sands of time. These became the arrows pointing the way to new goals and fresh objectives. We refer cynically to the "horse and buggy days." Yet, if there had been no horse and buggy, there would have been no automobile and no jet. We refer romantically and condescendingly to the "surrey with the fringe on the top." Yet, had it never been invented, many of our luxury modes of transportation would not have been possible. Galileo's footsteps pointed the direction for Newton, even as Newton's pointed the direction for Einstein. Memories are not mere fantasies or poetic illusions. They are the patterns of the past, which succeeding generations fashion into new forms and new achievements. These achievements represent progress. Our sages might have had that in mind when they said, "Memory induces action." [4]

Let us personalize this thought and recognize its relevance to our individual lives. Day after day another success story makes the pages of the public press. A new industrial tycoon appears on the horizon, and a success-conscious society stands in admiration before him. Then as the story unfolds, we learn

3. Hor. 13b.
4. Men. 43b.

that an immigrant father carried a heavy pack on his shoulders and trudged from village to village to sell his wares. Who knows but that the memory of the father's industry and frugality provided the incentive for the son's success.

A medical genius discovers an antitoxin that will save the lives of millions of children and protect countless others from the crippling effects of Polio. A grateful world stands in awe and reverence before a medical savior. Then we hear of an old-fashioned parent stooping over the machine in his humble tailor shop to enable a promising son to go to college. Might not the memory of a father's perseverance and self-sacrifice have inspired the son? The father bowed over a garment; the son assuming the same posture over a microscope!

A young Joseph in a strange Egypt is sorely tempted by Potiphar's wife. He resists temptation because, according to our sages, he beheld the image of an old father and recalled the moral instruction that he had received. In the end he rises to be vice-king of Egypt. Memories led to a throne.

The progress of each and every individual is in one way or another assisted by such memories. In a deeper sense we are all the products of such memories. Consciously or unconsciously, we "remember the days of old," and are the better for it.

There is another reality about memory that we would do well to recognize. Without memory, hope is impossible. Often in life tragedy strikes at our door. The incurable illness of a child, the death of a parent, a heroic son reported killed in action, a life's fortune lost overnight—these are not uncommon occurrences. Suddenly a dark cloud descends upon us and seems to blot out all light and all hope. Then, as calm settles over us, reflection begins. Others have lost fortunes and regained them. Millions of sons were reported killed in action, and millions of parents lived on. Death claims all, but life inevitably continues. When reality turns bitter, memory provides a measure of sweetness. And out of the sweetness is distilled hope and courage. Where there is no past, there is no future. Where there are no yesterdays, there will be no tomorrows. Where there are no memories, there are no prospects.

Some years after the destruction of Palestine, Rabbi Akiba and his colleagues walked across the hill whereon once stood the Holy Temple. Suddenly they beheld a fox emerging from the Temple ruins. The sages wept at the sight of desolation. Rabbi Akiba, according to the story, laughed. He explained his strange behavior by saying that, if God's prophesy of doom over Palestine came true, so would the promise of restoration come true as well. "Akiba, you have consoled us," said his grateful colleagues. Memory instilled hope.

By the waters of Babylon sat our ancestors and wept. Their land lay waste. Their sovereignty was lost. Their sad fate was cruel exile. All about them lay the harps of the Levites that once rendered sweet music in the Temple courts and now were muted. "How can we sing the Lord's song in a strange land?" they asked in despair. Then, as a mighty host they rose and solemnly exclaimed, "If I forget thee, O Jerusalem, may my right hand be forgotten." Through every exile, in every ghetto, in joy and sadness, at the bridal canopy and at the threshold of the crematorium, a people remembered the glories of its past, the promise of its Prophets, the assurance of its God. What a miracle this memory wrought! After eighteen centuries and more a state was re-established, exiles were gathered in, sovereignty was restored, and a driven people was rewarded—for its memory.

Never, as long as there is life within me, will I forget what I beheld in one of the displaced persons camps after Europe's liberation. It was in the Rothschild Hospital of Vienna, which served as a transient camp for refugees from Poland on their way to the American Zone. A transport of survivors had just arrived. What a sight! Those poor emaciated bodies, the orphaned children, the bereaved parents—all fugitives of hate and horror!

In one of the dark and dank rooms in which sat huddled some of the unfortunates, I beheld on one of the wooden cots an object that was not strange to me. It was a *shtreimel*, that ceremonial headpiece worn by the Jewish aristocrats at all religious and festive occasions. Near it sat its owner, an old, worn and bowed man. "Have you any other belongings?" I asked him. He shook his head. "Is that all you could save?" I inquired. "All that I wanted to save," he replied. "Why, why this?" Then came the unforgettable explanation: "All that I had was taken from me—my wife, my children, my home, my fortune, my synagogue, my books. All that I *had* was taken. But not all that I *was*. And this *shtreimel* is a symbol of what I once was. It is the memento of my former status. What I *was* no one can take from me, and what I was I shall one day be again."

This, my friends, is what memory does. Fortunate is the man who can repeat the poet's thought:

> *"Only stay quiet while my mind remembers*
> *The beauty of fire from the beauty of embers."* [5]

Fortunate is he who, with David, can say, "I remember the days of old."

It is impossible to conclude this thought without one further observation. For the Jew, memory is known by yet another name. That name is tradition.

For many, memory is a flashback from the past; to us it is a hand-down from the past for the endless future of our people. Others merely recall; we receive.

"Remember the Sabbath day to keep it holy." This is a command to remember. But is it only that? Of course, the

5. Masefield, John: *On Growing Old.*

Sabbath is a lovely, a romantic, even a dramatic memory—a clean tablecloth, candles, traditional dishes, perhaps even a family melody. Let no one minimize that. At best, however, this is merely a Sabbath—Jewish style. But the Sabbath, in addition to being remembered, must be observed. It is a day of rest, a day of holiness, a day in the course of which man transforms himself from mere creature to human being and from human being to Jew. Our sages would have us believe that when, at Sinai, God commanded, "Remember the Sabbath day to keep it holy," those who were there simultaneously heard a voice, which said, "Observe the Sabbath and sanctify it . . ." [6] Remember and Observe! Memory became tradition.

"Remember the day that you left Egypt." Again we are bidden to remember. This time we are asked to recall bondage, suffering, indignity and a host of other misfortunes that are the portion of a slave people. But here, too, that isn't all. The memory of Egypt imposes a commitment to freedom, a concern for the downtrodden, an interest in the enslaved, an eagerness to "proclaim liberty throughout the land and to all the inhabitants thereof." Here we have memory at work. When that happens, memory becomes tradition.

When children in Tennessee have to be led to school under guard of bayonets, the heart of a Jew is stirred. When the temple of education, the most precious sanctuary of democracy, is defiled by segregation and polluted by discrimination, then the Jew, whether Northerner or Southerner, ought not to rest without exerting every effort to cleanse and to purify the minds and the hearts of his fellow Americans. To recall Egypt, that is memory. To abolish all the Egypts, now and forever, that is the command of tradition.

"Remember the day when you stood before your God at Sinai." What a magnificent drama took place there. There was thunder and lightning and all the sound effects known

6. R.H. 27a.

and not yet known to modern impresarios. A people stood in awe, shook and shuddered before a spectacle of Revelation never previously performed, never to be repeated. But what took place at Sinai was more than a memory to be deposited in the mental archives of a people. There was an exclamation, "We shall do and we shall listen." By that act of commitment the memory became a tradition, binding upon the Jew to all eternity.

> *"Hail, Memory, hail! in thy exhaustless mine*
> *From age to age unnumber'd treasures shine!*
> *Thought and her shadowy brood thy call obey,*
> *And Place and Time are subjects to thy sway."* [7]

This is a poet's insight into memory. This, indeed, is memory transmuted from vision to action, from hindsight to foresight, from dream to reality.

O for the art of memory! Almighty God, on this Day of Remembrance, among all the other blessings, grant us this one —never to forget to remember.

7. Rovers: *Pleasures of Memory.*

Part III

Basic Human Needs

15 ❦

The Good Life

There is one prayer which, like a refrain, will recur throughout the High Holy Day liturgy. It is the prayer for life. We
will address God as "the King who delights in life." We will
implore Him to "remember us unto life." We will, of course,
hope that He will "inscribe us in the Book of Life." All of our
devotions at this season will, in effect, be variations on the
general theme of life.

The desire for life cannot possibly be a desire for mere existence. It is true that man is in constant terror of the ultimate
and that he is obsessed by a morbid fear of the grave. He loves
to believe that "death will be banished forever" and that he
may be spared "seeing the pit." Yet he seeks more than mere
existence.

Man is not content to shuttle the threads of being back and
forth upon the loom of existence. He would prefer to weave a
pattern and to create a design. He is not satisfied to respond to
God's roll call of the living with a feeble and anguished
"present." He would dare to ask the Almighty for more—
"Inscribe us in the book of *good life.*" [1]

The problem that confronts us, therefore, is—what is a
good life? When each of us addresses his appeal to God for an

1. Liturgy.

123

inscription in the "book of good life," what kind of response does he expect?

Perhaps it would be well to approach this problem by stating at the outset what does *not* constitute a good life. It most certainly is not the life of indulgence. In every period of human history, in one formulation or another, it was proposed that the optimum program for living is expressed in the slogan, "Eat and drink, for tomorrow we shall die." This is the hedonistic view of life. It is generally associated with early man in his primitive state. But it manifested itself in many periods of man's odyssey on this planet. We pride ourselves that civilized man has long ago abandoned that view.

But has he? Are there not many, even in our own day who, in Rousseau's strange statement, consider the ideal life as "a good bank account, a good cook, and a good digestion." That, of course, is a very crude way of putting it. Let us, therefore, transpose it into a more recognizable idiom. When we speak of a high standard of living, what do we mean? To some it is a chicken in every pot and a car in every garage. To others it is a fat envelope, with substantial take-home pay. To many it is a television in every room, well-stocked deepfreezers, and homes with wall-to-wall carpeting. To all of us it is high employment, a reasonable cost of living index and a wide variety of consumer goods.

Let us reflect a moment. Those two words, *consumer goods,* seem to be a subtle intimation of what the ideal of our day is. What is good? Whatever can be consumed. The quest for pleasure and its attainment, maximum satisfaction of desires, the abundance of creature comforts, the achievement of social success and economic security—put them all together and they spell out the modern conception of the *good life.*

To be sure, this view of the good life has its consequences. These consequences are discernible when, for example, one studies the problem of delinquency. There was a time when delinquency was associated exclusively with slums and poverty and underprivilege. Today, alas, we have learned that moral corruption, the use of narcotics and the disintegration of personality may be associated with overindulgence, even as with deprivation. We call them delinquents when they come from the underprivileged. We refer to them as "spoiled" when they hail from the overprivileged. In the one case, need and want are responsible; in the other, over-abundance and over-gratification are responsible.

At the opposite pole of indulgence stands denial. An entire philosophy was built around this conception. Life is sinful and evil. Beat it, therefore, at its own game. Practice repression, abstention and, if need be, total withdrawal. Flee from it; seal yourself off hermetically from its lusts and passions; and hide where life cannot get at you.

Judaism not only dissented from such a view; it considered it sinful. The Nazarite or ascetic who took the vow of abstinence and self-mortification was considered a sinner ". . . for he sinned against his soul," [2] and the Talmud explains that the sin consisted in that he imposed affliction upon himself through abstention.

Judaism takes the reverse view. It not alone sings with the poet that "life is real, life is earnest, and the grave is not its goal;" but it adds—life is beauty, life is joy, life is holy. The Jew is bidden to partake of food, of drink, of love, of pleasure. Even for those foods which are forbidden, our sages provided permissible substitutes. "Go eat your bread in joy and drink your wine with good cheer." [3] There is an obligation to enjoy life.

When others contended that it was better to marry than to burn, the Jew countered with the exhortation to "enjoy life

2. See Ned. 10a on Deut. 6:11.
3. Eccl. 9:7.

with the wife whom thou lovest." [4] We repudiated the morbid and melancholy and denied the crown of saintliness to those who escaped from life or sealed themselves off hermetically from society. Even God cannot reside in an atmosphere of gloom.[5]

This leads us to the first criterion of the good life. Neither escape from life nor absorption in it are the means by which ideal living may be achieved. Neither indulgence nor denial are the keys to real fulfillment. The magic word is *balance*. Balance is to life what symmetry is to art, what rhythm is to the dance, what harmony is to music. Without balance one may reel through life like a drunkard, stumble through it like a weakling or flee from it like a coward. Without balance, life is lopsided, and he who lives so is devoid of poise and grace.

One arrives at this conclusion out of a realization that life is not monolithic but variegated, not uniform but diverse, not consistent but paradoxical. Within the span of a single lifetime, how varied are the moods, how incongruous the experiences. Wealth and poverty come on the heels of each other. Failure and success appear cyclically. Birth and death arrive often simultaneously. Tragedy and triumph frequently intermingle. The stock market of life is never steady. It is nervous and fluctuating. It is sometimes "bearish" and sometimes "bullish," and often both at the same time.

> *From fibers of pain and hope and trouble*
> *And toil and happiness—one by one—*
> *Twisted together, or single or double,*
> *The varying thread of our life is spun.*

If this be life, then the good life consists of blending all these contrasting colors, shades and moods into an organized medley. He who balances the good against the evil, the hope

4. Eccl. 9:9.
5. Sabbath 30b.

against the despair, the laughter against the tears, the dreams against the disappointments, and makes the transition from mood to alternate mood—he who does this bravely and ungrudgingly lives the good life.

History abounds in glorious examples of such living. The once rich and happy, but then stricken and suffering Job could rebuke his complaining wife and say, "Shall we take the good from the hand of God, but not the evil?" [6] The triumph of Job consisted in his capacity to maintain a balanced life. He proved his ability to pass from wealth to poverty and back to wealth; to proceed from health to crippling illness and back to health; from joy to misery and back to joy. His was a good life.

"Give me neither poverty nor riches . . . ," prayed the author of Proverbs, "lest I be full and say who is the Lord, or lest I be poor and steal and profane the name of my God." [7] Is it hard to recognize personalities all about us who failed to understand that? Prosperity softens and spoils them; adversity embitters and crushes them; and the transition from one to the other engenders either greed or gluttony or frustration.

The biblical portion for this Holy Day provides an interesting example for our thought. Hagar is the character in mind. According to tradition, she was the daughter of a king or chieftain. Reduced circumstances compelled her to take a job as Sarah's handmaiden. How she must have chafed under that ordeal. Then, in accordance with the practice of the day, she became Abraham's concubine. She bore him a son. From princess to maidservant to expectant mother was the saga of her brief life. How did she take this change of fortune? "And when she saw that she had conceived," the Bible recounts, "her mistress was despised in her eyes." [8]

Here was a lady who apparently could not make a graceful

6. Job 2:10.
7. Proverbs 30:8.
8. Gen. 16:4.

transition from adversity to prosperity. Read what follows. She fled from Abraham's home; she returned; she gave birth to the child; she fled once again and wandered aimlessly in the wilderness. And then, "when the water was gone from her pitcher, she cast away the child under one of the shrubs . . . and sat herself down . . . and wept." [9] So, as long as there was water in the pitcher, everything was "fine and dandy." When there was no more, then came bitterness, tears and despair.

How many of us can recognize counterparts of such behavior? Business is good; profits are high; inventory is low— in a word, there is water in the pitcher. So we go merrily along on the highway of prosperity, confident that this state of affairs will continue indefinitely. Then something happens. Investments decline; profits diminish; prosperity vanishes— the water is gone from the pitcher. Like Hagar, we no longer find joy in our home, delight in a child that needs our love, and interest in a society of which we are a part. We retreat into ourselves, lost in the wilderness of our own confusion, and weep. If our depression is not too deep, we may be directed to the psychiatrist's couch, in the hope of finding relief and understanding. Actually, however, our trouble originates in our incapacity to lead a balanced life, to maintain proper poise and perspective, and to make the transition from stage to stage, from experience to experience, with courage and with grace.

Is not this thought confirmed by the most distinctive ritual of this day, the sounding of the Shofar? There are three dominant notes that issue forth from the ram's horn. There is the joyous blast of victory, the sharp wail of defeat, and the quivering groan of misery. These, my friends, are symbolic of the moods of life, the conditions of existence. To give a balanced tonal quality to each of these is to achieve a

9. Gen. 21:15.

harmony—a harmony which is symbolized by the *Tekiah Gedola*—the ultimate triumph of the good life.

There is another quality that characterizes the good life. It cannot be lived in isolation. It must be shared with others. Fundamentally, that is why the indulgent life and the ascetic life can never qualify as being good. The indulgent man thinks of no other. The ascetic man runs away from all others. The one is greedy in the physical sense. The other is selfish in the moral sense.

Our sacred literature reports an imaginary conversation between Noah and Moses. Noah contends that he is greater than Moses, because God saw fit to save him from the destruction of the flood, whereas Moses, on the other hand, was forbidden to enter the Promised Land. To which Moses replies: "You saved yourself, while your generation perished. I died in the wilderness, but my generation entered the Promised Land." [10]

It is ever thus. "Only a life lived for others is a life worth while," said the immortal Albert Einstein. The good and righteous man conceives his goodness in terms of what he can do for others. So Moses pleaded, "Let Moses die and a hundred like him, but let not the finger of a single Jew be hurt."

Is it not remarkable that when we appeal to God to be inscribed in the Book of Good Life, we say: "Inscribe *us* in the Book of Good Life." Not *me*, but *us!* This is the glory of Judaism and its mark of supremacy. It never stressed personal salvation. It teaches and strives for social salvation.

Our tradition teaches us that on this day of judgment the Jew must pray for the well-being of all mankind. Examine our liturgy. "Lord our God, inspire . . . veneration for Thee in all Thy creatures . . . may they all become one fellowship, to do Thy will with perfect heart." Read further.

10. Yal. Deut. 951.

"Who is like unto Thee, merciful Father, who in Thy compassion rememberest Thy creatures for life."—Not Thy people alone, but *all* Thy creatures. Read still further. "As a shepherd musters his sheep and causes them to pass beneath his staff, so dost Thou pass and record, count and remember every living soul."—Not every Israelite, but every living soul. We exclude no one from salvation. "The righteous of all people have a share in the world to come," [11] is the verdict of our sages. We are admonished that "whosoever saves a single life, it is as though he saved the entire world." [12] The good life can never be self-centered. It must be social centered.

In all languages of the world, the word "life" is a singular noun. In all languages except Hebrew! In the sacred tongue of our Bible and prophets, life is "*hayim.*" It is a plural form, and there is no singular for it in the holy tongue. Why? Because a good life cannot possibly be lived in the singular. It must be in the plural.

It now should be apparent that the good life is not achieved by praying for it, but by laboring for it. It is not the gift of God; it is the creation of man. God does not give it; man chooses it.

One of the great principles of Judaism is that man may exercise free choice. At birth he is not stamped, as others would have it, with the stigma of Original Sin. As he emerges into life he is neither good nor bad. Only the physical conditions of his being are imbedded within his genes. His moral character becomes his own business. "To be or not to be," that is for God to decree; to be good or not to be good is for man to determine.

"Behold, I have placed before you this day life and good, death and evil . . . Do thou choose life." If this verse means anything at all, it means that God is the author of life, but man must write the commentary on it. When, therefore, we

11. Sanh. 105a.
12. Tosefta Sanh. Ch. 13.

pray to God to inscribe us in the Book of Life, we are acknowledging God's authorship. When we qualify the request by expecting Him to inscribe us in the book of *good* life, we are evading a responsibility which is exclusively our own.

Similarly, we may appeal to God for the material conditions of existence, health, strength, abundance. These gifts are His to bestow. What we do with them depends entirely on us. He may settle us in an Eden of abundance and place at our disposal "every tree beautiful to behold and good to eat." It is we who fall prey to the wiles of the Serpent and surrender to the blandishments of the Tempter. He can give us a world of staggering dimension and of endless wealth, with room for all in it. It is we who in our envy and passion become the Cains who slay their brother Abel. "Behold, I have placed before you this day life and good, death and evil. . . Do thou choose life."

Modern man may well ponder this thought. The new psychology and psychiatry may have given him some erroneous notions. Too many of us fallaciously feel that we are now relieved of all responsibility for our action and conduct. Let us be done with blaming every abnormality and all neurotic behavior upon our grandmothers. To be sure, there are pernicious influences in the environment that affect us. Of course, there are festering cesspools within the soul of man that began in childhood and which, over the years, distorted and polluted his personality. Most of us, however, are mature and normal, and all of us can with effort rise to our full stature as men and women. Most of us are capable of the right choice. If we do not choose the right and the good, it is primarily due to the fact that we do not choose to choose.

Perhaps, then, our prayer on this day ought to be slightly revised. Inscribe us, O God, in the Book of Life. Enable us to provide balance and stability to that life. Permit us to share that life with others. Make us understand that such a life can be our choice. If we choose wisely, it will be a good life.

16

The Need to Belong

A little child, separated from his mother during the London bombings, reacted to his situation in the following words: "I am nobody's nothing." [1] This child intuitively enunciated a profound psychological truth. Each and every one of us wants to be somebody's something. There is a deep emotional need to belong.

This need we express in a prayer which, like a refrain, is repeated throughout the High Holy Day liturgy. "Cast us not away from thy presence." [2] It originated with David. When he first uttered it he was the absolute monarch over all Israel. His dominion was extensive, his possessions unlimited and his power unchallenged. Then he stumbled and sinned, and the prophet Nathan did not spare him in his scathing denunciation. David's atonement forms one of the most touching pieces of religious literature. He was prepared for any punishment, however severe. But there was one punishment he sought to avoid. "Cast me not away from thy presence." He wanted to remain somebody's something. He needed to belong.

This immediately emphasizes an important truth. Material

1. Freud, Anna: *War and Children*, p. 85.
2. Psalms 51:13.

possessions do not necessarily determine a sense of belonging. People all about us provide the evidence for that. Many things belong to them, but they belong to no one. Their material foliage may be rich, but their roots are not sunk deep in the soil of life. When the storms of existence begin to blow, the fragile stems of their personality bow, bend and sometimes break.

Who are some of the victims of maladjustment, of insecurity, of loneliness and of fear? Are they always the poor and underprivileged? Indeed, not! It may be a child brought up in wealth who, in the paraphrased lyric of an old song, senses that his heart does not belong to daddy. It may be a gifted and promising young man who pathetically regards himself as a member of the "lost generation." It may be an affluent father who suddenly realizes that his home is no longer his castle. It may be an outwardly well-groomed wife who inwardly is broken because she feels unloved and unwanted. It may be a retired old gentleman who, his physical usefulness ended, sees himself as a problem to all about him and to the new science of Geriatrics. A sense of belonging has nothing to do with what a person *has*, but with what a person is. It is derived, not from possessions, but from being possessed. "Cast us not away from thy presence."

This naturally brings us to a second thought. Our age seems to discourage a sense of belonging. Examine the literature of the day, the titles of current works, the slogans of our society, the standards of our culture. A young Englishman wrote a book last year, called "The Outsiders," which created a stir in the world of letters. He describes the intellectual, standing as it were, on the periphery of life and observing it, not as a participant, but as a spectator. The Outsider, even if he be an intellectual, is either a beggar or a hobo. Neither one has a sense of belonging.

Consider the vocabulary of our times—rugged individual-

ism, self-determination, The Lonely Crowd, the lost generation, the disinherited, the displaced person, the escapee, the
refugee—what do they all indicate if not a severance of the
roots of belonging. In a sense, our whole civilization is in danger of becoming one huge Displaced Persons Camp.

We are not entirely to blame for this condition. Technology has something to do with it. We will all readily agree that
the home and the family are the primary elements in personal
identification. Your address, father's name and mother's name
appear on every possible form or legal instrument, from a
driver's license to a marriage license, from a birth certificate to
a death certificate. We belong to parents before we belong to
any agency in the world. The first soil that our tender roots
strike is the home. Our first anchorage is at a mother's bosom
and our earliest mooring is a father's lap.

To get away from all that was no easy matter in the days of
the horse and wagon. Travel was difficult and attended by
hardships, even dangers. Highways were unsafe; movement
was slow, and new destinations were veiled in mystery. When
God said to Abraham, "Get thee out from thy land, from thy
birthplace and from thy father's house . . . ,"[3] it was a
command, considered by our sages as one of the trials and
tests of Abraham. A journey was a wrench, an adventure, a
plunge into uncertainty.

People, therefore, remained anchored and struck deep roots
and developed an intense sense of belonging. A primitive Cain
was crushed when he heard that he was doomed to be a wanderer and vagabond. A dejected David complained at his sad
fate, which was ". . . to be driven away from abiding in the
inheritance of the Lord."[4] People hesitated to be set adrift.
They wanted to belong.

It is different in our day. People, young and old, are anx-

3. Gen. 12:1.
4. I. Samuel 26:19.

ious to get away, and technology helps them. They jump into their roadster, hop a plane, pack a train case, and in a matter of minutes they are miles away "from their land, their birth-place and their father's house." They can even "travel now and pay later."

As for young people, they look forward to the out-of-town college as a pious Jew to the Messiah. The latter seeks escape from Galuth; the former seek escape from home, from hearth, from parents. In recent years, military life, formerly the occupation of the professional soldier, has become a seri-ous dislocator of young people, not without damage to their sense of belonging and peril to their emotional life.

The twentieth century is a very mobile one. It is not only on wheels; it is jet-propelled and before long rocket-driven. Modern man is in danger of forgetting his home address, and his sense of belonging will be attached to a name plate, marked "General Delivery."

Now, let no one minimize the importance of travel and the value of new places, the thrill of new sights, new people and new experiences. As a result of our mobility, our horizons have been widened, our judgment of others has been broad-ened, our sense of kinship with mankind has been deepened, and our hope for "one world" has been greatly advanced.

Let no one, however, overlook the fact that certain valu-able assets are lost in the process. Some very precious concepts disappear along the modern highways—the old homestead, old friends, old traditions, yes, even "the old folks at home." All these are ties to the past, roots in the soil of yesteryear, anchors to which we latch our sense of belonging.

A beauty queen was deprived last year of the crown that her comeliness entitled her to wear. Her disqualification re-sulted from her concealing the fact that she was married and the mother of two children. How pathetic! The ties of moth-erhood and the bonds of wifehood were not sufficiently strong. The glory of home and children was eclipsed by the glamour of Hollywood beauty queendom. Reports have it that she has since been divorced. The bow attached to the trunk of belonging broke. Down came beauty queen, children and all.

It is just to avert such tragedies that a sense of belonging must be cultivated—and in our days strengthened and fortified. In these explosive times people tend to be repelled, to be diffused, to be driven from secure moorings. Iron curtains separate us from our fellow man. Competitiveness is so fierce that sharp practices replace time-tested principles. Fears, real and imaginary, assail us. The old, we think, is not good enough, and the new we are not sure about. The core of personality is subjected to the relentless impact of trauma after trauma. Like the physical atom, it is ultimately smashed and it explodes in a cloud of emotional devastation.

In such desperate times man needs something to cling to. He needs the propinquity of his fellow man, else he will perish in lonely isolation. He needs the guidance of old principles, lest he get lost in the trackless jungle of life. He needs the inspiration of timeless traditions if his heart is to retain its human warmth and even beat. He needs the security of a home, which Robert Frost defines as the place

> *". . . where, when you have to go there,*
> *they have to take you in."* [5]

He needs roots so that, in the language of the Ethics of the Fathers,[6] if all the winds of the world blow upon him, he cannot be stirred from his place. In a word—he needs to belong. "Cast us not away from thy presence."

We may now consider the next thought. If the need to belong is so essential to man, then he will satisfy it in one way or

5. Frost, Robert: *The Death of the Hired Man.*
6. Ethics of the Fathers 3:22.

another. If he will not belong to what is good, then he will belong to what is evil. If he cannot belong to God, he will join hands with the devil.

There are ample examples of that if we but recognize them, and the literature of psychiatry is full of them.

What are gangs? They are associations of those who have been deprived of or denied more natural, more basic and more sympathetic forms of association. The home is uninviting; the neighborhood, a slum; parents are missing; yet the human heart craves companionship. It will grasp it wherever it can find it and will use it on whatever terms it demands.

What is delinquency? It is the revenge of social outcasts upon a society that cast them out. An adolescent who needs roots badly suddenly finds them cut. He is a black boy in a white society. He wants to belong and he is segregated. He is a recent immigrant who left his roots behind him and did not yet grow new ones. He is a youngster frustrated and rejected. His capacity for love turns to hate. His heart freezes up. Human emotions are suppressed and the animal in man stalks out from its subconscious lair. This is a candid camera shot of the soul of a delinquent.

What is communism of the Russian variety? It is man seeking an association, even if that association means enslavement. The process is as simple as it is ruthless. Family ties are weakened; the home is no longer a haven of love; fundamental beliefs are debunked; religion is represented as an opiate and God as an anachronism. The individual is shorn of his basic attachments. His roots are chopped from under him, one by one. He topples over and falls into the cruel clutches of the slave state and its tyrants. He needs to belong, if not to God and not to man, then to the devil.

What was Nazi totalitarianism? It was a people turned into a gang. Cunning leaders, who understood well the emotional need to belong, exploited that need to the utmost. They

offered defeated and frustrated people membership in an illu-
sionary super-nation. Mature individuals were induced to
regress back to childhood, to worship a *Fuehrer* as a glorified
father and to believe the infantile notions of perverted propa-
gandists. Millions were regimented to obey and to die. A
goose-stepping gang of hoodlums came near extinguishing
Western Civilization. The need to belong became a lever in
the brutal hand of a tyrant, and he used it with devilish
cunning. We have still not cleared away the wreckage that he
left.

This need to belong is of special concern to us as Jews. We
belong to one of the oldest peoples on God's earth. We are
the bearers of a tradition that has survived for more than
three thousand years. We can trace our ancestry back to an
Abraham who brought monotheism to our world. Our Ten
Commandments are the Magna Charta of civilization. We
gave a Holy Bible to the world. In it were first enunciated the
noblest doctrines of mankind. Here are some of them: Man's
dignity is inviolate—"For in the image of God did He create
man." Slavery must be eradicated—"Proclaim liberty throughout the land, to all the inhabitants thereof." Justice is the cor-
nerstone of civilization—"Justice, justice shalt thou pursue."
Personal morals distinguish man from the beast—". . . what
does the Lord require of thee but to do justice, to love mercy
and to walk humbly with thy God." Social ethics transform a
wilderness into a kingdom of God—"Have we not one father,
hath not one God created us, wherefore shall we deal treacherously with each other?" [7]
Our prophets were the first to envision universal peace and
world brotherhood. They designed the finest pattern of human conduct. Our poets sang to God and hungered for His
presence. Our seers preached to man and lifted him from the

7. Malachi 2:10.

mire of animalism to the heaven of human supremacy. Our sages taught and compiled a Talmud, the oldest and most complete codex known to man, the richest repository of law and lore. Our philosophers propounded the lesson that man is free to choose; that his fate is his own to determine; that existence is not darkened by the gloom of Original Sin; that sin is natural and repentance possible; that life is beautiful and the grave is not the end of man born in God's image. Our tradition insisted that knowledge does not contradict faith; that learning is a religious duty; that study is a form of worship.

Whosoever has his roots sunk in such a culture is drawing upon the sources of eternity. He belongs to a people and a way of life that confer upon him the crown of priesthood and the sceptre of a spiritual royalty.

This people and those who remained attached to it survived for three millenia. They outlived the ancient empires that sought to destroy them. The cramped ghetto with all its humiliation could not crush them. Medieval darkness did not extinguish the inner light of their courage, and modern gas chambers could not choke their indomitable determination. The fires of the inquisition and the flames of the crematoria could not consume them.

To belong to such a people is to sink one's personal roots into the inexhaustibly rich soil of Israel's being. To cling to it with all our heart, with all our soul and with all our might is to absorb Israel's strength and to acquire its courage and indestructibility.

Some of us are not aware of this. We, therefore, sever some of the strands that bind us to our people. We weaken our religious ties. We reduce our cultural commitments. We evade our philanthropic responsibilities. When considering the education of our young, we are prepared to settle for the minimum. "Jewish style" becomes the compromise for kosher diet. Israel, we conclude, is a foreign state and Zionism, we are afraid, is hyphenating our Americanism. The sight of a bearded Jew makes us self-conscious, and spoken Yiddish makes us squirm. A Jewish Day School, we fear, is self-imposed isolation, and spoken Hebrew evokes a condescending and patronizing smile.

Some, of course, proceed much further in the cutting of their Jewish roots. They become totally assimilated. Many German Jews once attempted that, and some in our own day refuse to learn from their tragic example.

Then comes the inevitable awakening. A restricted hotel refuses to honor our reservation. An academic quota prevents the admission of a son to a particular college. An exclusive fraternity or sorority does not "rush" the ambitious child of a social-climbing parent. The experience of anti-Semitism, whether in its overt variety or of the "Gentleman's Agreement" variety, suddenly confronts us. We are puzzled and humiliated and feel rejected.

The consequences are not easy to take. The old roots of belonging are either withered or cut. An individual is left in emotional isolation and solitude. He is neither a full Jew, nor a partial anything else. He is nobody's nothing.

The solution? It is intimated in the story of Jonah, which we will read on Yom Kippur. Recall that Jonah was a stowaway on a storm-tossed boat. He was fleeing from God, from his people, from his country, from his duty. All his ties were snapped; all his bridges burnt. Then the storms of life began to rage and the hurricanes of existence to howl. His fellow travelers, who up to then ignored his presence, suddenly became aware of him. "Tell us," they said, "are you not to blame for this trouble? What is your occupation, where do you come from, what land is yours, what is your people?" [8]

How many times in our sad history were these questions asked? Who are you? Who are you? To retain our equilib-

8. Jonah 1:8.

rium, to preserve our balance, our mental health and our emotional stability, let us answer this question without hesitation, without fear—and with pride. I am a Jew! Take it or leave it. I am a Jew! Whatever the consequences, my dignity is intact; my faith is firm; my honor unsullied; my pride is strong.

This is what a sense of belonging means. O Lord, "Cast us not away from thy presence."

17

The Need to Believe

The subject of belief always belonged in the realm of religion. Of late it has found its way into the domain of psychiatry. We have begun to suspect that to believe is more than a pious obligation; it is also an emotional necessity. The need to believe is no longer regarded merely as a matter of theology; it may well be an aspect of mental hygiene. We are beginning to wonder whether the Psalmist was not right when he said, "I have chosen the way of faith." [1]

It was not always thus. The eighteenth century witnessed the coronation of Reason as king, and the centuries that followed worshipped faithfully at Reason's throne. Our own Thomas Jefferson expressed the prevailing attitude. "Your own reason," he said, "is the only oracle given you by heaven." Faith was either entirely eclipsed or, at best, subjected to the relentless rationalism of the day. *Die Religion der Vernunft* or *The Religion of Reason* expressed the temper of the times.

What happened to God in the process? The title of a recent best-seller describes his fate—*Remember Me to God*. God was abandoned without even a fond farewell. Or he was so mutilated that he ceased to be God. He became a "con-

1. Psalms 119:30.

cept," a "category," a "supreme intelligence"—everything and anything except the God of Abraham, Isaac and Jacob, the God to whom one can call in perplexity, before whom one can pray in adversity and upon whom one can lean in sorrow and in anguish.

This is what happened to God. But what happened to man? The Age of Reason begot what came to be known as the New Humanism, and the New Humanism made man "the measure of all things." Man's economic needs, his material wants, his creature comforts, his political aspirations, his intellectual enlightenment, yes, even his sexual urges, became the preoccupation of philosopher, social scientist and psychologist.

But if man is the measure of all things, then he is more than is encompassed by this schedule of needs and wants. He is more than stomach, and hence "does not live by bread alone." He is more than a bundle of desires, and can, therefore, crave "that which his soul loveth." He is even more than mind; he is also soul. He has fears and anxieties. He is assailed by doubts and uncertainties. He is exposed to the desolation of wars, the ravages of disease, the torment of mental illness, the dread of loneliness and the monotony of boredom.

To be sure, man is wise and becoming increasingly wiser. But the increase of knowledge has also brought the inevitable increase of pain. He knows all about inter-continental missiles, atomic radiations and hydrogen bombs. Science has provided him with charts and statistics, and he knows how many will die of cancer and how many will be disabled by heart disease. Man knows all that. But he is now seeking not only more knowledge, but more support. He is looking not for a teacher, but a shepherd—one who will enable him to lie down in green pastures and lead him beside still waters and restore his soul. Most of his needs having been satisfied, there is yet one that remains unrequited—the need to believe.

Let one reassuring point be made at once. It is not difficult to believe. Indeed, it is easier to believe than to doubt. It was Emerson who said, "We are born believing. A man bears beliefs as a tree bears apples."

We do not realize how true that is. Long before we learn to reason and to understand, our lives are conditioned and molded by beliefs. Our very birth into the world is the result of a man and a woman reposing trust in each other. The security of childhood derives from belief in the strength and wisdom of parents. As we grow older we develop confidence in a father's guidance, in a mother's love, in a teacher's instruction, in a wife's fidelity, in a friend's loyalty. Our entire life is but a progression of beliefs. When the Psalmist said, "I have chosen the way of faith," he must have meant just that. Life is a way of faith, a highway paved with the bedrock of belief.

This brings us to another truth. It is not only natural to believe; it is also imperative. Without belief, life is impossible.

Without belief, progress most certainly is inconceivable. Newton believed Galileo even as Einstein believed Newton. One scientist did not have to check the equations of another. He believed them, and proceeded from that belief to develop a new set of equations.

Two brothers believed intensely that under certain conditions the laws of gravity could be overcome. Out of that belief was born the plane, the jet and the rocket into outer space, with all its possibilities as yet unforeseen. Long before the microscope detected them, Pasteur believed that minute invisible creatures existed, and the science of medicine was revolutionized. A Freud believed that many important secrets lie hidden and locked in the subconscious recesses of the mind, and mental therapy in all its forms came as a blessing to mankind. In a world of idolatry a young Abraham dared to believe in one God, and monotheism began to eclipse paganism.

From the lime pits of Egypt an aroused Moses fled. But he believed in freedom and justice too much. So, fired by that belief, he returned to emancipate a people and ultimately to "proclaim liberty throughout the land and to all the inhabitants thereof." Such is the progress that belief brought.

"Strong beliefs bring strong men and then make them stronger," [2] said a wise social philosopher. "A man of belief shall abound in blessings," [3] says Scripture. No beliefs—no blessings and no progress.

Let us carry this thought one step further. Without belief, society is impossible. Life would be a jungle, and the world a wilderness. There was a time when it was so. The stranger was always suspect; the newcomer was regarded as a potential enemy. When two strangers met they would embrace each other, not as a sign of affection, but as assurance that there were no concealed weapons upon their persons. The outstretched hand offered similar assurance. Such was the life of primitive man and the complexion of savage society. Where there is no belief, there is suspicion. Without trust, there is treachery. Where there is no confidence, there is fear. "Help us, O Lord . . . when belief is vanished from mankind." [4]

Let us narrow this thought down a bit. Let us bring it closer to home. And I mean this not figuratively, but concretely. See what havoc can be brought when faith departs from our homes.

There is a current best-seller with the strangest of titles—*Where did you go? Out—What did you do? Nothing.* What a tragic title! It pronounces the indictment of a generation. Children have lost faith in parents and will not confide in them. Parents have not justified their children's faith; they have let them down and have lost their parental authority

2. Bagheot, Walter: *Physics and Politics*, p. 76.
3. Psalms 28:20.
4. Psalms 12:2.

over them. The home which always exuded warmth, which resounded with laughter, which provided security, which bestowed love, which cultivated respect has, alas, in too many instances become a place of fear, of suppressed hostility, of sullenness and of gloom.

Why is it so, we wonder in despair. Where have we failed, parents ask in bewilderment? There are, of course, many answers. But one basic cause dare not be overlooked. Fundamental faith has departed from the home. Basic beliefs are no longer cultivated in it. Our children hear too much about the almighty dollar and too little about Almighty God, too much about pleasure and too little about values, too much about fashions and too little about manners. Americans spent last year more than a billion dollars on toys. How much have we spent on religious education? What great books are to be found in our homes? And do we read them, or are they merely part of the decor of the living room? Is the voice of prayer heard in our homes—the blessing before food, the grace after meals? Do we set the proper example of humility and gratitude and reverence? "O Lord, help us, for belief has vanished . . ."

Let us now expand the scope of our reflection and proceed from our private homes to our collective home—the world in which we live. See how it is divided into East and West, into black and white, into Jew and Christian, into Israeli and Arab. Two major wars in one generation has been our fate. Several smaller wars followed and endless cold wars continue to plague us. Suspicion is rampant; fear is unbridled, jealousy unchecked and hostility persistent. Why, O God, why? Because, except in the House of God, we never ask this question of God. We consult every substitute god for an answer—the political scientist, the economist, the statesman, the diplomat. Well, what have *these* gods wrought? See the mess we're in!

How shall we emerge from this mess? Many answers are

offered. Control the atom, establish free trade, internationalize outer space, help the underdeveloped areas—these are some of the answers, and they are undoubtedly valid. But these solutions will prove futile, nor will we ever adopt them, unless we first recognize and abide by certain basic premises. There is a moral law superior to every other law. Principles supersede profits. Ideals are often stronger than weapons. Human values are more precious than oil. Honesty, and not expediency, is the best policy.

Perhaps the world should give thought to a Summit Conference composed, not of generals and presidents, not of premiers and prime ministers, but to one of an entirely different character. A Summit Conference is needed with Him who is truly at the summit. "Help us, O Lord, for belief has vanished from mankind."

A concluding word must be spoken. Without belief there is no hope, and without hope life is intolerable. Reality is often so bitter and hard to take. Whenever encountered, it seems so decisive and final. In personal life it can shatter and crush—a child crippled by polio or handicapped by mental illness; the head of a family disabled by heart disease; death in the midday of life, which parts loved ones forever. Many of us are no strangers to these.

In our collective life the encounters with reality are no less traumatic—the cruelty of men, the chronic evil of the world, the betrayal of friends, the ruthlessness of enemies, the annihilation of wars and the threat of new ones. All of us are familiar with these and with what they do to us. When we experience such reality we seek frantically for help. What support does Reason offer? It tells us that this is the scheme of life. What strength does science contribute? It explains the inherent logic of our problems. What consolation from philosophy? In the darkest hour of mankind's misfortune it spawned the indifferent and harsh doctrine of Existentialism. It tells us that existence is hard, that man is unregenerate, that God is unconcerned, that fate is sealed and that ultimate salvation will come—after death. An interesting and eloquent commentary on our times is that an Existentialist man of letters, Albert Camus, was awarded the Nobel Prize in literature.

What, on the other hand, has true religion to say to man in his desperate dilemmas? What, for example, does Judaism offer us in our despair?

Forgiveness!

> *"Though your sins be as scarlet they shall become*
> *white as snow."* [5]

Confidence!

> *"Trust in the Lord. Be strong and let your heart*
> *be firm. Yea, Trust in the Lord."* [6]

Consolation!

> *"Comfort ye, comfort ye, my people, saith the Lord."*

And Hope!

> *"And they shall beat their swords into plowshares,*
> *And their spears into pruning hooks,*
> *Nation shall not lift up sword against nation,*
> *Neither shall they learn war anymore."*

Let our sophisticated generation smile at these sentiments if it wishes. Let it call them religious sedatives or theological barbiturates. Of course, they are not that at all. What are they? They are beliefs, and beliefs are the affirmations of the soul. The mind has its affirmations and the soul has its own. A sophisticated generation which simultaneously happens to be a crisis generation needs both. "Help us, O Lord, when belief is vanished from mankind."

5. Isaiah 1:18.
6. Psalms 27:14.

Out of the concentration camps which disfigured the landscape of Europe emerged a most unusual tale. Humans were being herded into cattle cars on their way to extermination. Wails and cries rent the heavens. Suddenly there was a hush, and high above the sobs and screams a different sound was heard. It was a melody beginning in a minor key and gradually changing into a major one. It was a dirge slowly transposed into an athem of triumph. Arms were locked and a ring was formed. Shadows began to sway, then to move and finally to dance and sing. This was the dance of the doomed, the ballet of the dying. What were they saying? What was the strange lyric of this fantastic song? Listen to it: "I believe . . . in the coming of the Messiah."

Out of Auschwitz and Treblinka, out of Dachau and Bergen-Belsen, from every slaughter house in Europe, came an affirmation of man's unconquerable faith and of mankind's inevitable triumph. "I believe . . . in the coming of the Messiah." Such is the hope that was inspired by faith. It led from concentration camp to the statehood of Israel, from gas chamber to freedom, from crematorium to redemption.

This heroic faith is the spiritual and intellectual legacy of our ancestors to us and to humanity. By such faith we too can be redeemed.

18 ❦

The Need for Serenity

The greatest need of modern man is serenity. Materially, all seems to be well with him. Prosperity is at an all-time high. Business is good. The general economy is sound. The standard of living is constantly rising. Creature comforts were never more abundant.

And yet, we are somehow disturbed, tense, anxious and afraid. The batteries of our personalities are supercharged, and in the inwardness of our life there is no serenity. A biblical metaphor describes our condition well. Modern man has the green pastures all right. What he desperately needs is the still waters to restore his soul.

This brings us at once to grips with our theme. Serenity is a condition of the soul, not of the body. It is an inward mood and not an external posture. The Psalmist put his finger on it. "Wherefore, O, my soul, are you disquieted, and wherefore do you moan?" [1] He, too, suffered from inner turmoil. He had conquered his enemies, extended the borders of his land, won the allegiance of his people and secured the monarchy for the son of his choice. But his spirit remained troubled, and his soul continued its plaintive lament. Serenity was, alas, denied him.

1. Ps. 42:12.

One admission must be made at the start. Our times are not conducive to serenity. Our world is extremely noisy, full of clamor and tumult. Every metropolis is engaged in some form of anti-noise campaign to reduce the blasting and blaring, the grinding and grating, which form the raucous cacophony of our day.

Try to preserve a mood of serenity in such a world, many will argue. The argument is incorrect. For even were we to seal ourselves off from all the din and discord about us, our problem would still remain. Because silence does not necessarily beget serenity, and quietness does not produce tranquility. The soul is not affected by acoustics. Serenity does not require soundproofing.

Let no one misunderstand. There is no suggestion here that serenity should be sought for as an end in itself. Neither should sleep be regarded as an end in itself. But as one wise preacher put it: "Sleep is a grand place to start out from in the morning." [2] So is it with serenity. It is a great thing to start out from. It is a precious and indispensable tool of life.

Most people recognize that. So, feeling the lack of the genuine tool, they attempt all sorts of unavailing substitutes. Thirty-six million prescriptions for tranquilizers were written by doctors in one year. Thirty million Americans now buy one billion and two hundred million tranquilizing pills a year. Drug addiction is on the increase, especially in the forty-year age group, an age when life should be most buoyant and satisfying. But, can sedatives generate serenity? Can L.S.D. induce a lasting inner calm to a harassed spirit? "O, my soul, wherefore are you disquieted?"

Others try to escape from their inner turmoil by recklessly plunging into all kinds of thrills and excitements, from alcohol and gambling to infidelity and sensuality. Even the young get

2. Dr. Harry Emerson Fosdick, in a sermon entitled "The High Uses of Serenity."

carried away by this rash and restless search for "kicks" of all sorts. Look about you and see the dress and hair styles. Observe the weird "beatniks," and listen, if you can, to the orgiastic rantings of the "beatles." This kind of escape simply will not work. The small still voice will continue to ask hauntingly, "Wherefore are you disquieted?"

When the plunge into pleasure and thrills proves futile, the heart returns to its emptiness. Clouds of depression descend upon the soul. Man is left to struggle in loneliness, to suffer the torment of relentless agitation and to endure in darkness the tortures of pitiless frustration. Here is one such person speaking to his friend, who became his biographer: "What does a man care about? Staying healthy. Working good. Eating and drinking with friends. Enjoying himself . . . I haven't any of them, do you understand, . . . none of them."

This from a Nobel Laureate in literature, Ernest Hemingway. Alas that such a talent found no other solution to life, except death. Alas and alas that such a spirit was not blessed with serenity.

There are more than twenty thousand suicides in the United States every year. Dr. Paul Friedman catalogues the factors responsible for the suicidal act in the Encyclopedia of Mental Health. He lists among others, incurable disease, loneliness, sexual betrayal, loss of status and pessimism about one's future. But, he observes, ". . . many more people undergo such suffering and affliction without ever attempting suicide."

The truth of the matter lies in what one of those unfortunates wrote: "No one thing is responsible for this and no one person—except myself." Phrase it whichever way you like; this person and others like him did not possess serenity.

Well then, what can we say to our harassed and harried generation? How can we direct those who crave for it, to the still waters that restore the soul? Where lie the sources of serenity?

For one thing, there can be no serenity without love. Love is more than the theme of the poet and the ideal of the romantic. It is not the passion of the lustful, nor even the symbol of the mystic. In the language of Erich Fromm, love is "the answer to the problem of human existence."

Most psychologists now agree, and teachers of religion concur, that love is "relatedness." Man is a lonely creature in a hostile world. All his misery and anguish are the result of the existential loneliness. Love is the magic key which opens the doors of his prison and releases him from his solitary confinement. He can then emerge to enjoy the freedom of nature, the companionship of his kind and the fellowship of society. Through love he overcomes his apartness and separateness and, overcoming them, ceases to fear and to tremble. Love or perish, says modern psychology. The Jewish sages said it better: "Companionship, or death." [3]

Love, so understood, is really part of the scheme of life. Nothing exists in isolation. That is as true of man as it is of atoms. The late Joshua Liebman, in a book published posthumously, put it beautifully: "Carbon atoms form charcoal when related in one way and become diamonds when related in another."

"Man," say our sages, "was born alone." [4] But in his aloneness he was only half a man. When out of his ribs God excised the one who became his beloved, He really did not diminish man, but completed him. [5]

How poetically Shelley expressed this philosophy of love:

"The fountains mingle with the river
And the rivers with the Ocean,

3. B. Taanith 23a.
4. B. Sanhedrin 37a.
5. Gen. R. 17:2.

The winds of heaven mix forever
With a sweet emotion;
Nothing in the world is single;
All things by a law divine
In one spirit meet and mingle.
Why not I with thine? . . ."

Only in a heart filled with such love can serenity dwell. Serenity cannot coexist with hate, neither within a single personality, nor within a world community.

Look at many of our homes and try to recall the homes of our childhood. Those old homes did not have wall-to-wall carpeting and all the other features of comfort and elegance that distinguish the American home. But of the old home one could say, in the idiom of Solomon: "Its interior was paved with love." In it children saw the love of a husband for a wife, and it gave them a sense of security. They felt the love of parents for them and reciprocated in kind. *Sholom bayis* was part of the interior decor. The home was a sanctuary of peace, a temple of tranquility. We did not own cooperative apartments, but we had cooperative homes.

Look outside the home into the teeming cities of our country. One can almost touch the brooding hostility that erupts recurrently into violence. "Black Power" and "White Racism"—what are they if not festering foci of irrepressible and explosive bitterness? The air of America is being polluted, and all of us—black and white—are inhaling contamination. Snarling hatred by one side and spiteful vengeance by the other will not beget racial equality or civil rights. Only one thing will do it. Love! The kind we all know but refuse to recognize. It comes not from the Emancipation Proclamation, nor from any manifesto of the Negro people. It is the old, unimprovable "Love thy neighbor as thyself." No love—no racial peace and no serenity for anyone.

There is another obstacle that man must overcome if he is to enjoy the serene life. It has many names, mostly ugly ones. Let us call it by the most euphemistic one—insatiable ambition. Such ambition is at the root of man's restlessness. It drives him relentlessly, afflicts him physically, disturbs him emotionally and robs him of all inner peace.

Our competitive society is, of course, partly to blame. But it is man who contributes and succumbs to such a society. We are paying a dreadful price for all this. Every time the market goes down, blood pressures go up. The incidence of coronary thrombosis has become the barometer of business success.

Associated with ambition is, of course, jealousy, envy, covetousness and greed. Sometimes ambition takes the form of social climbing and status seeking. So many things we desire, we really have no need for. But others have them and, therefore, so must we. We are the supreme "wanters" of the universe, according to one preacher.

A cartoon I once saw comes to mind. It shows a man in a magnificent store, in which beautiful and costly things are displayed. But the man does not look at them. He is totally indifferent to all the costly splendor about him. The caption of the cartoon reads: "Freedom from Want." Oh, if we could have such freedom! What serenity would be ours!

When we have made love an indispensable ingredient of our lives and when we have successfully curbed our insatiable ambitions, there is still a task before us if we are to achieve inner calm. We must look to our social relationships. How do we react to others? For man can never be at peace with himself if he is at war with his fellow man.

Too many of us try "to bite the world." To avoid that, we must acknowledge certain things. No two men are alike. God created us all different. "Even as their faces are not alike, so are their traits not alike," [6] say our sages. God created man in His image; let no man try to change that image to his own.

Parents sometimes try to do just that. They would force their children to conform to the pattern that they designed for them. Husbands frequently forget that wives may have their own individuality and that love does not mean surrender. Wives are hurt because a husband does not seem to measure up to a particular romantic image that they prefer. And the "angry" men of the world tyrannize nations and force upon them a uniformity that stifles character and destroys human dignity. Man cannot goose-step his way to progress.

There is no serenity in a police state. Absolutism is a curse upon the soul of him who inflicts it, no less than upon the victim. Men were created equal but not the same. No two flowers have the same fragrance; no two snowflakes have the same design, and no two personalities are cast in the same mold.

Translate this thought into universal terms and you have one of the most desirable principles of human conduct— tolerance. The parent who is intolerant is an unhappy parent. The religious bigot who will not allow "each man to walk in the name of his God," is insecure in his own faith. The anti-Semite is a sick soul. The totalitarian is ridden by fear and anxiety. And those of us who are convinced that they are always right and others are invariably wrong, are more wrong than they realize. If they bludgeon and bully to impose their view and will upon others, they are doubly wrong. For they indicate thereby that they are not sure of themselves and are afraid lest others discover it. Such fear and such anxiety do not make for serenity.

Our thought would not be complete without this final word. Serenity is hardly possible without a sturdy faith. Love

6. Num. R. 21:2.

is, of course, essential. The curbing of insatiable ambition is necessary. Respect for the sacred dignity of man is imperative. And yet, for the heart to be truly serene, man needs moral support. This is provided by a great faith. It is what one clergyman called, "the invisible means of support."

Here is an illustration of what is meant. A little boy was flying his kite on a cloudy day. In the darkness there was no sign of the kite anywhere. Only the long string could be seen reaching up and disappearing in the mist. "Why fly a kite you can't see?," he was asked. "Oh, but I feel it pull," he answered. This is what a great faith does. It pulls. It guides. It directs. It steadies.

All of us must learn this. The United States Department of Commerce recently reported that some ten cents of every dollar spent by the public goes for clothing, accessories and jewelry. Six cents goes for recreation. Three cents for alcohol. Only one and a half cents is used for religious and welfare activities. Might it not be that that is why we are only one point five serene?

Our tradition tells us that the first man was created on Rosh Hashana. What is suggested here is that man has an annual opportunity to be recreated and transformed. To each one of us that can happen, even this day.

The first man was called Adam. How shall we address the new man in each of us? May I propose an old salutation that goes back to the days of chivalry: [7] "Your Serene Highness." Yes, so shall it be—"Your Serene Highness."

7. Dr. Harry Emerson Fosdick uses this thought in his sermon, "The High Uses of Serenity."

19

The Way to Happiness

The traditional greeting for this season is "A Happy New Year." The very fact that this greeting is universal is an intimation that the experience of happiness is by no means universal. Alas, that is indeed so, especially for our generation. With the Psalmist, all of us are inclined to say, "Gladden the soul of your servant." [1] All of us crave a happy new year!

Outwardly we appear to be quite happy. Sports events are well attended. Entertainment has grown into a huge industry. In fifty million American homes old and young are laughing over the antics of television comedians. Restaurants are crowded; bars are full; cruises are booked solid. All of us seem to be whooping it up and joining in the refrain of a revised lyric: "I want to be happy."

It does not require much introspection, however, to realize that all of this is superficial and that our happiness is not really genuine. In the privacy of our lives there is gloom. If we could translate our mood into language, we would probably resort to the plaintive passage of Lamentations: "The joy of our heart is ended . . ." [2] To be sure, there is merriment, joviality, even gaiety, but not "joy of the heart."

1. Psalms 86:4.
2. Lamen. 5:15.

158

And how can it be otherwise in this messy and muddled world, racked with fear, distracted by suspicion and embittered by hostility. How many wars—cold or hot—can one generation endure without havoc to its nervous system? From the Congo to Cuba and from Siberia to Suez rage the hurricanes of hate and terror. The heavens above us blink with ominous satellites, and the earth is stockpiled with atomic warheads. Is happiness possible under such conditions? Listen well, and above the count-downs at launching platforms, above the taunts and threats of evil men, you may hear the sob of a scared generation which prays: "Gladden the soul of your servant." Oh, how badly we need a happy new year.

Well, then, where lie the groves of happiness and by what road does one reach them. In a word, how can one attain happiness?

Perhaps one ought to begin by stating how happiness is *not* attained. Happiness does not result from the possession of material things. Oh, how many of us can testify to that! Tell me, dear friends, how much does one have to possess in order to be happy? How rich does one have to be in order to be wealthy? Or, as we used to say when we were children, how high is up? Is it not apparent that the possession of things is never a barometer of happiness?

Besides, if we conclude that possession is a standard of happiness, are we not reducing man to the level of the beast? Listen to a philosopher of the eighteenth century decide that happiness is "a good bank account, a good cook and a good digestion." Not so, Mr. Rousseau. That may apply to a cow, not to the human species. A good stall, a fertile pasture and a healthy stomach will make for a happy cow, not for a happy man. Long before Rousseau, a Jewish thinker temporized with that mood and in Ecclesiastes said: "There is nothing under the sun better for man than to eat and to drink and to be merry." ³ Well, was Ecclesiastes happy? Was he not the melancholy cynic whose morose philosophy was, "vanity of vanities; all is vanity?"

False, indeed, is the notion that happiness results from abundance, from material security, from physical satisfaction. And our generation will sadly attest to that. We have more wealth, more leisure and more comforts than any generation before us ever dreamed of. Why then, amidst all our bounty, do we have to be guided towards "Peace of Mind" and towards "Peace of Soul?" The national income of the United States last year was over 366 billion dollars. There are fifty million automobiles on the highways. Why, then, are psychiatrists so busy? Has the possession of things brought happiness?

Or look at the international scene. Russia can accommodate hundreds of millions more on her vast steppes and along her rich mountain sides. Australia, almost as big in area as the United States, has only eight million inhabitants. Brazil, bigger than the United States, has a population of only thirteen million. The Arab lands, immense and untractable, are rich in resources that have as yet not been touched. One would imagine that in a world in which there is so much wealth, so much space, so much untapped riches, there would be happiness and brotherhood and peace. Well, study the sullen faces of the motley gathering now at the United Nations General Assembly. Observe the strident and blustering behavior of power-hungry chiefs of state. Then try to sense the worry, the sorrow and the sadness of a scared humanity. Has the possession of things brought international happiness?

Turn, if you will, to our domestic life. Our homes are beautiful in their decor and luxurious in their comforts. Our children are permitted to enjoy every advantage of modern civilization, from an individual television set to guided tours

3. Eccl. 8:15.

abroad. Our national cosmetics bill is in excess of one billion dollars. All of this should make for happy homes and happy marriages. Why, then, is divorce so common? One out of every four marriages in the United States ends in divorce. Why are there so many problem children? Why so much delinquency in the rich, as well as in the poor, sections of our cities? In one year more than fifty thousand swimming pools were installed in the back yards of American homes.[4] Why, then, are our youngsters and their parents so bored amidst all this affluence? Does the possession of things spell happiness?

A recent advertisement described what the copy called "a happy family," standing before their long-long car and saying, "We're not wealthy . . . we just look it." Clever, indeed! But one might revise the copy to read—we're not a happy family . . . we only look it.

Perhaps if we shifted our attention from the accumulation of *things* to the perfection of *self*, we might draw closer to the source of true happiness. The prescription for happiness then becomes relatively simple. Be concerned less with *having* more; be concerned more with *being* more. The higher we mount on the scale of self-improvement, the further will we advance on the road towards true happiness.

The lives of the great provide ample illustration of this truth. One such illustration may be found in this morning's Scripture reading. Here is Abraham, brought up as a child in a pagan household. Not at all an ideal setting for a bright and sensitive youth. He recoils from the folly of idolatry and slowly begins to conceive the idea of One God. What an advance in self-improvement!

Presently, under divine compulsion, he is prepared "to leave his land, his birthplace and his father's home," and to set out a-wandering over Mesopotamia. Not a happy life—the

4. Packard, Vance: *The Status Seekers*, p. 22.

life of a nomad. But he was not a mere tourist in the Middle East. At every stage of his journey "he built an altar to God," and wherever he went "he called in the name of the Lord." This nomad *was* happy. He had embarked on what might well be called—Operation Self-Improvement.

His fortunes were hard, his disappointments many. The wells that he dug were stolen by greedy neighbors. His flocks were never safe. Even his wife was snatched from his side. When fortune smiled at him, it was for but a while. Came an economic crash—"And there was hunger in the land." A depression set in and the struggle began all over again.

Yet, when at one point, after a war that he waged to save a kinsman, his ally, the king of Sodom, said to him, "Give me the captives and take the spoils for yourself," this proud patriarch of our people refused. He would not take "from a thread to a shoe string." Why? Here at last was riches at his feet. Vast lands and grazing fields would be his. Why not, Abraham? All over Mesopotamia the news would spread—small-town boy from Ur rises from carver of idols to tycoon land-owner.

But that was not the ambition of Abraham, the founder of the Jewish nation and the earliest proponent of the One-God idea. He was not concerned with the possession of *things*, but with the improvement of self. He did not want to own soil. He wanted to grow a soul. His supreme moment was not when he reclined on soft Oriental carpets to quaff wine and to partake of fatted lambs. His supreme moment was when he stood before God and pleaded for justice, even for the wicked of Sodom.

Was a personality so radiant, so perfected, so ideal, happy? Well, let us see. He lived a full and rich life. When he died at a ripe old age he was, according to the Bible, "old and satisfied"—not only old, but *satisfied*. And the Rabbis add that at his death the great of the world stood bowed in grief and mourned, "Woe unto the world that lost its leader. Woe unto the ship that lost its pilot." [5] All had to acknowledge that true happiness is achieved through the cultivation of a noble being. "For I know him," said God, "that he may tell his sons and his household after him to keep the way of the Lord, to do righteousness and justice . . ." [6] Oh, how happy is the man of whom that can be said!

If we are prepared to recognize that happiness may be a-chieved through the perfection of one's self, then a second truth follows. Happiness may be achieved through the forgetting of one's self. Would that modern man learned this truth.

Some years ago the famous British philosopher, Bertrand Russell, wrote a book, the title of which was "The Conquest of Happiness." The very title is an error. One does not go out on a campaign for happiness. One does not pursue it, track it down and then capture it. As a matter of fact, one never really conquers happiness. He is conquered or overcome by it.

"In every part and corner of our life, to lose one's self is to be the gainer; to forget one's self is to be happy." When Robert Louis Stevenson said that, he was not aware that he was enunciating an old Talmudic judgment—that whosoever would truly live must subdue his self. [7]

People rarely realize this. So they go about in "pursuit of happiness." They pray to God for a happy new year. They seek the help of a psychiatrist to relieve their depression and to restore their happiness. They read books on how to stop worrying, how to attain peace of mind, how to acquire peace of soul. And the more they concentrate on happiness for themselves, the less likely they are to achieve it.

Why not reverse the technique? Suppose we start thinking

5. B.B. 91a.
6. Gen. 18:19.
7. Tamid 32a.

of the happiness of others, the peace of mind of others, the peace of soul of others. Here, for example, is the prophet's prescription for happiness:

> *"And if you draw out your soul to the hungry,*
> *And relieve men in misery,*
> *Then light shall dawn for you in darkness,*
> *And your dull hours shall be bright as noon."* [8]

What the prophet is trying to say is that the gloom in a person's soul can be dispelled by the light that he kindles in another's soul. Bernard Shaw, with biting precision, put it well: "We have no more right to consume happiness without producing it than to consume wealth without producing it." A slight commentary might be added: It is impossible to consume happiness without producing it. Happiness is the dividend that one receives from the investment he makes in the well-being of others. An act of kindness is performed, and the purveyor of the kindness is happier for the deed. A smile is brought to a sad countenance, and the glow of that smile is reflected in the soul of him who caused it.

> *". . . All who joy would win*
> *Must share it—Happiness was born a twin."*

This would be a much happier world if we recognized this truth—the truth which a social philosopher of the last generation so aptly formulated: "No one can be perfectly happy till all are happy." [9]

There would be lots more happier marriages and happier homes if we recognized this truth. Many a "misunderstood" husband would be far less misunderstood if he demonstrated a little more understanding for his partner in marriage. Many an unhappy wife would be far happier if she brooded less over *her* unhappiness and concentrated more on how to make

8. Isaiah 58:10.
9. Spencer, Herbert: *Social Statistics,* part IV, Ch. 30.

a husband happy. Young people would feel less rejected if they did not make their parents feel rejected. Parents would have less cause for disappointment if they, in turn, did not repeatedly let their children down. Happiness is not a one-way experience; it is a reciprocal experience. Invariably, it is the result of an effort to make someone else happy.

It should now be apparent, and that may well sum up our thought, that happiness is not something that you seek, but something that you find. It is not an end, but a consequence; not a goal, but a by-product of a certain way of life.

The very vocabulary associated with happiness emphasizes this thought. One does not "go in" for happiness as one "goes out" for a good time. To "do the town" is characteristic of one who is pleasure-bound. To do something with himself is the exercise of a person whose ultimate reward is happiness. "Enjoy yourself, it is later than you think," sings one whose desire is merriment. Bring joy to others is the advice of one who has learned the true secret of happiness.

Happiness, then, is the result of two efforts that seem on the surface paradoxical, but are not. It is determined, first, by what a person does with himself; by the extent to which he improves himself; by the good that he distills out of himself. It is achieved, second, by a person's capacity to forget himself through absorption in the happiness of others.

We pray for and we wish each other "a happy new year." And we seem to forget that in the Jewish tradition there is no such prayer or greeting. Our prayer and greeting is *Leshona Tova*, which means *A Good Year*. The intimation is clear— without goodness there is no happiness. Oh God, grant us a good year. A happy year we shall find on our own.

20 &

Where There Is Hope
There Is Life

When Jeremiah wrote, "My strength is gone, and my hope in the Lord," [1] he really provided the text for pessimism at its lowest. His words may well be used by the prophets of gloom that abound in our generation.

Let us at once admit that it is not easy to be an optimist these days. Pessimism is more in keeping with the mood of the world. The smoke of Hiroshima and Nagasaki has by no means cleared. It hangs like a pall over our generation, and its fall-out has infected the hearts and spirits of men with sadness and fear.

There were more than eight million dead in the First World War. In the Second World War the number rose to twenty million. Even twenty years after the close of hostilities, cities all over the world still show the ugly scars of ruthless bombings. Can one be optimistic in such a world?

The Middle East and the Far East are strained with tension. Asia and Africa are boiling over with revolution. In the jun-

1. Lamen. 3:18.

gles of Vietnam, innocent and unnecessary blood is being shed in a war which no one seems able to explain and no one knows how to end. To escalate or not to escalate, that is the question! Before an answer is found, untold numbers will die and millions will brood in gloom. Against such a global background, pessimism is natural.

It is understandable, therefore, that some apostles of pessimism are ready to throw in the sponge. They are prepared to ring down the curtain on the human drama. There just seems to be no hope for man, they feel.

Men of letters like Kafka, Sartre, Camus and Andre Gide, portray man as lonely, sad, lost and hopeless. The Surrealist artists paint man in waxen colors, with eyes that are empty sockets. The sculptor's mallet hammers out angular and ungraceful figures that make man look like a scarecrow. Even the music of our day is without theme and form, so that the conductor as he directs seems to have St. Vitus' dance and the sounds that come forth are more like groans and death rattles.

The song of our day is set in a minor key. It is not an epic of triumph, but an elegy written in a universal graveyard.

There is a touching parallel to all this. When the first man saw his first sunset, he was frightened and said, ". . . Woe unto me, the world is turning into darkness and soon will become void and desolate . . ." But then he saw the dawn rise and said, "this is the way of the world." [2]

Hear this our pathetic pessimists. "This *is* the way of the world." If there is a chink in your personalities, do not, like Henny Penny in the Mother Goose story, go around shouting, "the sky is falling." And as for you shoulder-shrugging sophisticates, remove your dark glasses and correct your myopic vision. And you, our modern novelists, behold and describe the vast vistas of beauty, rather than the ugly alleys of filth. There are views other than The View From the

2. B.A.Z. 8a.

Terrace and places other than Peyton Place and valleys other than The Valley of the Dolls.

Here we encounter the most pernicious trait of the pessimist. He does not really see life; he sees only himself. Life to him is but a reflection of himself. If he has a jaundiced view of the world, it is because *he* is jaundiced. Perhaps Bernard Shaw was right after all. "Do you know what a pessimist is?," he asked. "A man who thinks everybody as nasty as himself and hates them for it."

The pessimist has no hope for man, because he has lost faith in himself. He sees no future for mankind, because for some pathological reason he wants no future for himself. He foresees ruin and destruction, havoc and catastrophe, because these are the punishments that he feels *he* deserves. In a word, pessimism is not a philosophy; it is a mental illness.

The pessimist does say, "My strength is gone, and my hope in the Lord." But he desires no strength and he believes in no Lord. Sartre, Camus and their melancholy company were all valiant fighters in the French underground. They saw the cruelty and brutality of man. They realized how feeble was their strength when pitted against the might of the tyrant's legions. They decided that God was indifferent, and they abandoned him, even as they thought he abandoned them. At war's end they emerged from their lairs, without faith, without hope and without God.

Young Franz Kafka was, without question, a genius, but an unhappy one. He feared and hated his father and his father's God as well. He was weak, sensitive, lonely and frustrated. "My strength is gone, and my hope in the Lord," might well have been an evaluation of his life. A brilliant mind wedded to a sick soul.

And so with many a pessimist. They cannot be understood except through the insights of psychiatry. Their bleak and black view of the world is but a copy of their own unhappy and frustrated personalities. Their canvas of life is dark, because they dip their brushes into the black pigment of their own spirits.

Our concern, however, is not with extreme and abnormal manifestations of pessimism. Normal people, too, are subject to pessimistic moods. They have reasonable doubts. They are afraid of failure. They question their own adequacy. All these are natural reactions. What can we say to such people?

What do we say to people who out of deep personal despair are moved to say, "My strength is gone, and my hope in the Lord"? All too often a rabbi hears the agonizing cry of parents for whom life has ceased to have meaning in the face of a child's hopeless physical or mental condition. How can we assuage their pain and restore purpose to their life?

And what of those whose pessimism stems from unfulfilled hopes and possibilities?—a young man who in the prime of life was struck down by disabling disease; a hopeful couple whose promising marriage ended in disaster; a happy family from which death plucked the choicest member. What can we say to all these?

To some of them there is little we can say except to help them discover inner spiritual resources and reservoirs of strength and hope. Others, we might persuade that sorrow and adversity need not be depressants. They can be goads and challenges, as indeed they were to many. The broad-jumper goes a few steps backwards to gain momentum for the leap forward. So is it with life. It pushes us backwards on our heels, and it expects us to jump forward on our toes.

But when we are all finished comforting and persuading, we can still be left with sympathy for those who have a right to feel that life has let them down. There are, however, those who slink into pessimism whom life did not let down, but who let life down. What shall we say to them?

The first thing is to draw the attention of the pessimist away from himself and towards others. Sartre has a play called *No Exit*. In it he has one of the characters say the following: "So this is Hell? I'd never have believed it. Do you remember all we were told about the torture chambers, the fire and brimstone? There's no need for red-hot pokers. Hell is—other people!"

There you have it! The pessimist is preoccupied with himself. He is his own little world. But even in this microcosm things can go wrong. It can be invaded by pain, sickness, sorrow and death. The little world is affected by economic upheavals, by wars, by crime, by racial injustice. It is then that the self-centered man, feeling threatened in his smugness, turns in bitterness against the larger world and pronounces its doom. When his own paradise is lost and he finds himself in the teeming arena of life, he imagines that he is in Hell. To him, "Hell is—other people!"

All of us abhor racial violence. We wish with all our hearts that such episodes as occurred in a Harlem public school this week may never recur. We would love to see an end to Freedom Marches and to banish white racism and its brutality. But shall we conclude that because these things exist, America is going to the dogs? Why? Because these things impinge upon *our* little world? Because they hurt *our* little businesses? Because they disturb *our* smug indifference or distract us from *our* little pleasures.

What are we prepared to do about all these evils that bewilder our country and the world? Life is with people, and those who recognize that, have no desire to be cynical, no need to be flippant and no time to be pessimistic. They are too busy helping people.

This should make the pessimist realize another important thing: All the business of life is done by the optimists. Pessimism is a form of paralysis. The pessimist is so busy complaining, criticizing and lamenting that he loses the inclination to act. His disposition is sour; his tongue is bitter, and his hands are lame.

One immediately thinks of an illustration from Scripture. Moses sent spies to explore Palestine. They returned with a glowing report. It is a land flowing with milk and honey, they said, and blessed with all natural resources. "But," they added,—the pessimist invariably interjects a "but"—"the natives are strong, the cities are fortified and powerful . . . We are not able to march against the natives, for they are stronger than we." [3]

Here is pessimism in action. Well, what followed? What followed is pessimism in inaction. "And the people wept that night . . . And they complained against Moses and Aaron . . . And they said . . . let us appoint a leader and return to Egypt." [4] A pessimist can cry. He can complain. He can wallow in the wilderness of his own misery. He can even return to the Egypt of the *status quo*. But he cannot go forward to the Promised Land of fulfillment.

Only the optimists are capable of that. The way may be hard. The prospects appear uncertain. Logic may not be on their side. But the will commands and the goal beyond beckons. So the optimist advances—and conquers.

It has always been thus. In the nineteen thirties of our day, democracy was under attack. It was considered flabby. It made men feeble and mushy. It put power in the hands of the weak. The doom of democracy was foretold.

Two alternatives were offered. One of them was heralded

3. Num. 13:27–32.
4. Num. 14:1–4.

as "the wave of the future," and even a famous American aviator and his wife espoused it. It was the glamorous, goose-stepping and brown-shirted Nazism of Hitler Germany. In reality, it proved no "wave of the future" at all, but a return to the jungle and a retreat to the beast in man.

The second alternative was to choose the new Utopia— Communism. Again a return to the fleshpots of Egypt, even if it meant a new serfdom.

Who were the champions of progress in those days and who were the saviors of democracy? A man in a wheel chair who told us that we have nothing to fear but fear. What an immortal optimist! Who else? A man in his seventies who offered his countrymen blood and sweat and tears. But the two fingers of his right hand that formed the letter, "V," inspired a nation to reach its "finest hour," and the world to march to victory. What an unforgettable optimist!

Who knows what the fate of mankind might have been had a tongue-tied and slow-mouthed Moses not lived. Paganism and idolatry might have continued for centuries. Slavery and injustice might have kept man in darkness and delayed the dawn of civilization.

But Moses did live. There were moments of pessimism in his life too. He complained bitterly: ". . . Why hast thou ill-treated this people? . . . Ever since I came to speak in thy name to Pharaoh, he has ill-treated this people, and thou hast done nothing to rescue thy people." [5]

Before long, this man of halting speech became a master of moral eloquence. "Proclaim liberty throughout the land, to all the inhabitants thereof . . . One law and one statute for the stranger and the native alike . . . Love the stranger . . . Love thy neighbor as thyself . . ." Only an optimist can overcome a speech impediment and become the emancipator of a people and the moral teacher of the world.

5. Exodus 5:23.

What made a blind Milton write and a deaf Beethoven compose? What made Helen Keller distill light out of her own darkness? What made all these fill our lives with poetry, with music and with beauty? Optimism—and the will and determination that it alone can generate! The pessimist is a critic and a destroyer; the optimist is a doer and a creator.

One cannot conclude this subject without observing that the Jewish people, too, is exposed these days to gloomy prophesies and to evil forebodings. From pulpit and platform come prognostications of doom. "The Vanishing Jew" has become the theme of rabbis, sociologists and communal leaders.

The symptoms are, of course, alarming. There is a falling birth rate among Jews. Inter-marriage is reaching frightening proportions. The free and open society in which most Jews now live is stimulating the process of acculturation. This results in a loss of Jewish identity, especially among the young generation. Eventually they fall victim to corroding assimilation and are lost to our people.

The lamentations over the condition are in a large measure justified. There is cause for concern and there is reason for anxiety. But jeremiads will not help the situation.

Judaism has been threatened before. The survival of our people was in jeopardy during many periods of our long history. The fascinating culture of Greece could not entice us away from our faith. The mighty legions of Rome could lay waste our land and set fire to our temple. But the Academy of Yavneh remained, and Rabbi Johanan ben Zakkai and his associates continued to teach our Law. In the dark ghettos of Europe the light of our culture continued to glow. The Crusaders could not destroy us, and the Inquisition could not convert us. Even in the extermination camps of Nazidom we continued to practice our faith. And when we emerged from them, bereft of six million of our kin, our very first act was to print a new edition of the Talmud on the printing presses of Hitler's Munich.

By the waters of many Babylons did our ancestors sit and weep. But soon they wiped their tears and began to plan "how they might sing the Lord's song in a strange land." And sing it they did, with sweetness and strength, and their children caught the melody, and it became a symphony of faith, of courage and of hope. This is the unfinished symphony of the Jew, and it will never be finished till the end of time. "I the Lord do not change, and you the sons of Jacob are not consumed." [6] This is the pledge of God and our assurance of survival. This is the source of our national optimism.

When a drama is ended and ere the curtain is lowered, the audience frequently calls, "Author," "Author." As the pessimists of life prepare to ring down the curtain on the human drama, and on the Jewish drama as well, let us stay their hand. Let us look up to Him who is the source of all confidence and call, "Author," "Author." Aye, where there is hope there is life!

6. Mal. 3:6.